Low Impact Living Communities

in Britain

Edited by

Sarah Bunker

Chris Coates

James Dennis

Jonathan How

A Diggers & Dreamers Review

DIGGERS AND DREAMERS PUBLICATIONS

Diggers & Dreamers
Publications
2014

First published
2014
D&D Publications
BCM Edge
London
WC1N 3XX

ISBN
978-0-9545757-4-8

Distribution
Edge of Time Ltd
BCM Edge
London
WC1N 3XX
020 8133 1451

Typesetting and Layout
Sarah Bunker
Jonathan How

Cover Illustration
Gill Barron

Acknowledgements: Thank you to all our contributors and to the many communities and other organisations that have responded to our requests for information. Once again we've been to several places for our meetings in the last two years, so grateful thanks to everyone at Redfield, Crookstock, Lammas, Birchwood, Beech Hill, Mornington Grove and LILAC.

Contents

Preface

DAVE DARBY

Director of the environmental organisation,
the Low-impact Living Initiative, LILI

I'm really excited by this book. For me, wanting to live sustainability is one of the most important reasons for being in a community. From an early age, I knew something was wrong. I used to love watching the beautiful David Attenborough programmes, but at the end it always said the same thing – these creatures are now fighting for survival, their habitat is threatened, etc. What was going wrong that meant we didn't seem to be able to share our planet with other species? We want it all – but of course we can't have it all. We need a healthy ecology to be healthy ourselves, and ultimately, to survive. Edward O Wilson, the world's most respected ecologist, tells us that at current extinction rates, we're set to lose half the world's species of plants and animals in the next 100 years. Half! And of course it won't stop there. It's very worrrying – an ecological crash will be much more damaging than an economic crash – and yet very few people know what's happening. It doesn't appear to be very newsworthy.

As a teenager I wondered why people didn't live together to share resources. Why do we need five washing machines between five houses, when one would do? The same goes for lawnmowers, garden tools, and maybe we could even share cars, clothes and books. People could get together to grow food, keep animals, plant trees, share chainsaws, tractors, power tools, maybe even share kitchens and bathrooms, make decisions together, teach each other skills, babysit for each other, install renewables, co-operate. I thought it was either a brilliant new idea, or a hopeless dream, but I was wrong on both counts. Aged 19 I discovered an organisation that sent people to work in the communal Kibbutz system in Israel. I'd never heard of the Kibbutz, had barely heard of Israel, knew nothing about the politics of the Middle East and had never been abroad. But I signed up and went to live on a Kibbutz for a year in my early twenties.

On the Kibbutz I heard about the International Communes Desk in Tel Aviv. I went there and browsed their library. I discovered communities all over the world, and scribbled down lots of contacts. Back in the UK I attended Middlesex Uni, and on a field trip happened to sit in the passenger seat of a minibus being driven by Dennis Hardy, who has an article in this book. I'd never been to his lectures, and didn't know who he was. I started talking to him about communities, and he told me that that was what he specialised in. I accepted his invitation to the annual conference of the International Communal Studies Association at Edinburgh University and met many more international communards (hello and thank you Dennis). I began to contact them to ask if I could visit and stay in exchange for food and somewhere to sleep, and in my late twenties, set off on a WWOOF-style trek (I didn't know about WWOOF at the time) around communes in Africa, India, Japan, Australia, New Zealand and all over Europe. Later I visited Ganas and Twin Oaks in the States too.

Rural communities can be stepping stones for people wanting to escape the city and/or corporate jobs, but lack the skills to move straight to a smallholding or a more naturally-inclined lifestyle. They can also be breeding grounds for new low-impact initiatives – course programmes, small businesses, networking, challenges to the planning system and environmental organisations like LILI.

I've heard people after attending LILI natural building courses say that they are now going to buy a few acres and build a natural home. They often haven't looked into it too deeply, and don't realise that they will come up against the might of planners who really don't want them to do that. The planning system has done a wonderful job stopping suburbia and industry from taking over the countryside – but low-impact living is different. As long as they abide by strict environmental criteria covering building materials, energy, water and what they do with the land, low-impact smallholders can enhance the ecology of the countryside by planting trees and hedges, and producing organic food for local markets. As well as being more sustainable, intensively-farmed smallholdings produce more food per acre than large monoculture farms.

The people at Lammas community in Pembrokeshire have set a precedent by persuading their local planners (after two appeals) to allow them to build homes on a 75-acre farm well outside any development zone, as long as they abide by very strict eco-criteria and a low-impact development policy that they had a hand in putting together. They've started building their homes and community hub, planting trees and hedges and producing food. They've also influenced the Welsh Assembly to introduce the TAN6 'one-planet' policy that should make this sort of project much easier to realise in Wales. Environmental awareness is much greater nowadays than when I watched David Attenborough as a child, but unfortunately the problems are much greater too. Developments like these, along with new urban housing co-ops and co-housing projects make me optimistic that we can turn things around, and that communities will have an important role to play in that.

To find out more about LILI, visit:
www.lowimpact.org

Dave Darby
founded the Low Impact Living Initiative (LILI) during the 13 years that he lived at Redfield Community in Buckinghamshire. He now lives in South London.

Introduction: Something has to be done

CHRIS COATES

Chris asks where low impact living has come from and where it might be going

Over the past two decades a new category of intentional community has emerged growing out of a wider new back-to-the-land movement, driven in part by the high price of rural housing and taking its name from what started out as an attempt to devise new planning criteria that would allow people to live and work in the countryside. Low-Impact communities, or Low Impact Development, as it is more widely known, was a phrase coined by Simon Fairlie in his 1996 book *Low Impact Development: Planning and People in a Sustainable Countryside.* In which he described it as a "development that, through its low impact nature, either enhances or does not significantly diminish environmental quality". Other names might have emerged to describe the variety of developments that now go under the 'Low-impact' banner – Fairlie himself considered various other options; Earthcare developments, sustainable developments... but it was Low-Impact Development (LID) that he chose – and the one that has stuck and has evolved in some places into a quite specific Planning-based definition. The book was written whist Simon was living at Tinkers' Bubble in Somerset, "... out of the frustration of trying to obtain permission to live in a self-built, off-grid community...", is part a history and philosophy underpinning the idea and part a how-to-find-your-way-round-the-planning-system manual for would be Low-impacters.

Since the publication of Low Impact Development, the concept and definition of LID has been refined and developed by various other people and groups and there has been a wealth of research projects and initiatives in support of low impact ideas and practice. In 1999 the Rural Planning Group of The Land Is Ours produced a list of 15 criteria by which LIDs could be assessed, and Chapter 7 was founded to lobby on behalf of low impact builders, smallholders, caravan dwellers and other low income rural people facing planning problems, and offering free advice. Also in 1999, Scotland acknowledged the existence and the potential benefits of low impact housing in its national planning guidance. Perhaps the most headway in getting a shift in official attitudes has been made in Wales. After a long, highly publicised planning struggle over the low-impact community at Brithdir Mawr, in the Pembrokeshire National Park, where the battle to prevent the demolition of Tony Wrench's Roundhouse became something of a cause célèbre and rallying point for the Low Impact movement, both the Pembrokeshire National Park authority and the Welsh Assembly have come up with working policies for Low Impact Development. Things have been slower to move forward in England, despite lobbying by Chapter 7 who, in 2003, published a 50-page document, Sustainable Homes and Livelihoods in the Countryside, advocating changes to the government's proposed planning policy statement PPS7 on the countryside. There is still very little, if any, planning policy at a national or local level that supports the idea.

While all this researching and lobbying was going on, increasing numbers of people were just getting on with it. Starting up their own low impact projects, both individual and collective, more often than not by just moving onto land they had bought without applying for permission in advance. Whenever any of these cases have come before a planning authority after initial refusal by the local council they have gone to appeal, and in the majority of cases appeal Inspectors have decided, on the face of the evidence, that they are a justifiable exception to local planning policies. In England, since 1999, almost every low impact community that has gone to appeal: Kings Hill, Tinkers' Bubble, Steward Community Woodland, Landmatters, Fivepenny Farm, Quicken Wood, Keveral Farm, has been given temporary or permanent planning permission. More recently, in Wales in particular, there have been moves towards working with the new low impact planning criteria. The Lammas project at Tir y Gafel, in North Pembrokeshire was set up with the aim of becoming a model that could be replicated across Wales. It combines traditional smallholding with innovative environmental design, green technology and permaculture ideas and gained planning permission in 2009. (See Paul Wimbush's article on page 87)

> *"Low-impact development will not really be able to explore its potential until it has government approval. People quite naturally want to work within the planning system and until low-impact development is redefined as lawful development it will remain a fringe movement. It is therefore imperative to create a policy framework that permits such development. To date Pembrokeshire is the only county in the UK with a fully fledged low-impact policy. Current indications from the emerging Local Development Plan would indicate that the future of this policy is currently in question. The importance of this policy for the low-impact movement cannot be understated."*[1]
>
> Paul Wimbush

It could be argued that there is nothing new in the idea of low-impact development. That not only have people all over the world been 'living low impact lifestyles in low impact buildings for centuries', but that there are also plenty of precedents within the intentional communities movement in the UK over the last 50 years. There have been numerous people quietly living in low impact 'housing' in the grounds of 1970's big house communes underneath the local planners radar for years. While in the past it has been an assumption that communal living was 'green' and that sharing resources with others was less environmentally damaging, there is actually very little statistical evidence to back this up one way or the other. About the only piece of research on the subject was done back in 2001 by Horace Herring[2] – who concluded that it was more the relative poverty, voluntary or otherwise, of the groups he looked at that reduced their environmental impact rather than communal living in itself. It would be interesting to see a comparison between the impact of an established intentional community and a newer low impact group. Could LID just be a rebooting of the 1970's self-sufficiency movement for the 21st century? Perhaps the big difference now is the attempt to get the LID concept officially

**Low Impact Living Community,
illustration by Catriona Stamp.**

1 Solar reflector cooker
2 Cooks take a break
3 Outdoor kitchen area

4 Homes built of local wood
5 Yurt
6 Solar powered laptop
7 Teleconferencing via VOIP
8 Pressing apples and bottling juice for sale
9 Grazing area

recognised within the planning system and with it open up the opportunity for more people to choose a less environmentally damaging lifestyle. There is even talk of Low-Impact becoming more 'mainstream' which does seem a tad over-optimistic given the difficulties experienced by any group in getting off the ground recently and the lack of any real engagement by officialdom. Though it does seem strange that at a time when environmental issues have crept up the political agenda that the practical opportunities for change offered by LID are not seen in a more sympathetic light.

"LID has huge potential to deliver truly sustainable development immediately, helping Britain feed, fuel and house itself. In addition to carbon positive, rather than carbon neutral development, LID can help both rural and urban regeneration. However, if LID is to be brought into the mainstream it is vital that LIDers themselves continue to set the agenda in terms of defining and expanding what LID is. This sets a significant challenge to the planning system tasked with working in participatory ways with people, with a minimum of bureaucracy. It also presents challenges to LIDers themselves to form new and innovative partnerships, working with more mainstream organisations such as Housing Associations, Local Authorities, charities, NGOs, researchers, schools, educators and enlightened building companies."

Larch Maxey[3]

In the pages of *The Land* magazine, which charts low-impact activity in the UK as well as other land use issues, you can see two distinct strands of low-impact development. On the one hand there is the lone individual or couple looking for a way to live on the land and perhaps work a smallholding or practice woodland crafts who face one set of planning hurdles and on the other hand the more organised collective (if not communal) projects that face a whole different set of hurdles not only planning, but constitutional, financial and interpersonal that they have to cope with. Recently Jenny Pickerell from Leicester University has had a go at trying to define specific criteria for Low Impact Communities rather than just a narrow a LID planning definition.

Low impact communities are those projects which:

1 Seek autonomy and self reliance, and thus seek to generate all that they need

2 Often have mixed goals but tend to include becoming more socially, economically and ecologically sustainable

3 Tend to share values. Some are thus intentional communities, others less so, but most have community agreements by which all occupants consent to

4 The ethos is self-build and do-it-yourself

5 Are structured around living and building collectively and often include sharing communal space

6 Involve a care and consideration for others. This can include deliberately seeking to reconfigure existing relationships, such as practising gender equality

7 Are low-cost and often build affordability for perpetuity into the long-term design

8 Can require a change of lifestyle and/or income generation

9 Seek minimal resource use (in construction and life-cycle)

10 Have low visual impact

11 Are built from local, recycled or natural materials

12 Are often small scale

Dr Jenny Pickerell[4]

Much of her definition would apply to many of the groups that have appeared in *Diggers & Dreamers* over the years and much of the 'soft-technolgy'; meeting techniques, work systems, resource management etc have been being trialled, used, developed, cast aside, picked-up and tweaked for decades in communal set-ups across the country. There is a wealth of experience that new LID groups could tap into. This book is an attempt to facilitate some of that cross-over of knowledge and experience.

"In the post-war decades popular mythology held that every acre of Britain was precious in the interests of agriculture. Farmers were free to destroy woodlands and hedges, drain wetlands and pollute rivers and water supplies in the interests of increased production. Now that the bubble of over-production has burst, the same people are subsidised for not growing and for returning habitats to what is seen as nature. This results in golf courses and publicly-financed set-aside.

Unofficial settlements are seen as a threat to wildlife, which is sacrosanct. The planning system is the vehicle that supports four-wheel-drive Range Rovers, but not the local economy, and certainly not those travellers and settlers seeking their own modest place in the sun. These people have bypassed the sacred rights of tenure, but still find their modest aspirations frustrated by the operations of planning legislation. Nobody actually planned such a situation. No professional planner would claim that his or her task was to grind unofficial housing out of existence, and nor would any of the local enforcers of the Building Regulations.

But all these unhappy confrontations are the direct result of public policy. Something has to be done to change it."[5]

Colin Ward

Chris Coates
is President/Chair of the International Communal Studies Association and author of *Communes Britannica: a history of communal living in Britain 1939-2000*. He is a founder member of Forgebank Cohousing project.

Notes

1   www.lammas.org.uk/oldsite/lowimpact/documentsLowImpactDevelopmentinWalesPaulWimbush2009.pdf
2   Does Communal Living Save Energy? Horace Herring. Paper to 7th International Communal Studies Association Conference, Zegg Community, Germany, June 2001.
3   Pickerill, J and Maxey, L *Low-impact Development – The Future in Our Hands*
4   Pickerill, J. 2012. *Permaculture in practice: Low Impact Development in Britain*. J. Lockyer and J. Veteto (eds.). Berghahn Books.
5   The hidden history of housing. http://www.historyandpolicy.org/papers/policy-paper-25.html

Words Are Not Enough

CHARLOTTE OLIVER

Charlotte gives a subjective account of her experiences at Landmatters Co-operative, a permaculture project in South Devon.

"Do you have any tips on how to design with a large group of people?" I would ask any permaculture teacher I came across.

This time, would it be the wry smile, the spontaneous laughter or something in between? It was the late 1990s, I'd done a Permaculture Design Course, formed a co-op with others and resolved to establish a low-impact permaculture community in South Devon. However, I was getting the impression that large-group permaculture design was not everyone's idea of fun.

I'd seen land squats and protest camps evolve with the guiding hand of permaculture, but their temporary nature demands different skills from the long-term, ecologically viable settlement we were envisioning. However, when it came to doing it for real a few years later, the smilers and laughers proved their metal and gave generously of their time, patience and skill to our fledgling group of landlubbers.

Buying the land (by what had become Landmatters Co-operative) had a gestation period of nine months between the bid and ownership. Much Visioning* was done, and drawn on paper, while small revelations were made of the visioner to the group.

*Throughout, capitalised words are permaculture terms.

Smiles of kinship – as the same Element in the same position on different pieces of paper emphasised the rightness of the whole – were punctuated occasionally by cries of alarm. "Is that really a prison you've drawn there?". This is the period of maximum freedom – every minute to be enjoyed to the full.

It is now ten years from those first tentative steps and the good folk at *Diggers & Dreamers* thought it about time we passed on some of our experience. They are not wrong. Because they have hit on the bete noire of permaculture design – Documentation. For this I recommend that any land-based group ensures one of its members is a creative type with a low-level obssession for order, who can't sleep until they have written, drawn or otherwise recorded and filed in a safe place the observations, processes and conclusions of the group.

We didn't but, nevertheless, Landmatters does have an impressive pile of dog-eared papers, half-filled notebooks and minutes of meetings that track our progress through the stages of designing the land and community at Allaleigh.

A permaculture design session

When we started in 2003 there were few low-impact settlements, and none consciously doing whole-site permaculture design. Permaculture is the glue that binds the group, and a design course certificate is a prerequisite for membership. We were a self-selecting group, and never did a formal Client Interview on ourselves. Being a dozen 'clients' who are also the dozen designers continues to boggle our brains. But the legal and bureaucratic necessities of buying land, registering the Rules of the Co-op, opening a bank account, applying for planning permission and simply being able to articulate what we were doing to friends and family, meant we had to nail a few statements of intent very quickly.

We adopted the Permaculture Association's definition of permaculture, and the *15 Criteria for Low-Impact Development* (published by Chapter 7), wrote policies on consensus decision-making, conflict resolution, transport, animals, live-in vehicles, biodiversity, residents, and visitors – all of which have endured and form the backbone of our collective lives.

Permaculture design begins with Observation. This is another stage to be relished for its freedom, but is often curtailed by other demands on people's time. Fortunately we were able to do it by the book and devote a year to this stage, noting the changes of season, the weather, flora and fauna, the spaces and people beyond our hedges, and our emotional responses, while changing nothing on the land.

The size and geographical spread of the group meant it took time to arrange meetings and make decisions, so the observations happened during regular 4-day visits – talking, eating and sleeping together in the communal bender on the edge of one of the fields. Solitary observation walks were pleasant respite, spiced with anticipation at being able to report something exciting.

But the time I felt most connected to the land in those early years, and learned the most of its rhythm, was in the second year when, before anyone lived here, we layed one of the long-neglected boundary hedges. Throughout that winter I took my billhook and bowsaw, picnic lunch and waterproofs to the hedge, from where I watched the comings and goings of the resident birds, foxes, mice, voles, rats and cats, learnt the feel of the bark and bend of the different hedge trees, the smell of the earth and the touch of the breeze that meant rain was coming. It was also a valuable time for making quiet contact with others in the group, and introducing friends to the nature of our new lives.

Fifty of the 200 pages of Aranya's excellent book, *Permaculture Design, a step by step guide* (published by Permanent Publications), is devoted to Site Survey and Mapping. This reflects the fact that design is largely about the positive Placement of Elements and the making and maintaining of Beneficial Relationships between them. Landmatters has some lovely maps, but I have to confess they don't look like Aranya's. They don't have overlays, baselines, contours and bearings, and to this day we remain strangers to the A-frame and bunyip.

To visitors I explain that if they are walking downhill they are going away from our living field, and uphill will return them to it. It's a principle we absorb through our bodies as we walk the land, and one we instinctively apply to the placement of compost heaps and rainwater tanks for example. Our feet have drawn the contours on the ground.

In our planning application in 2004 we explained that to do permaculture properly we needed to live on the land. We listed a multitude of good reasons, like integrating ourselves into the existing ecosystems, performing many diverse tasks during the course of a long day, and being able to demonstrate the low-impact lives we espoused. In retrospect, one of the huge benefits of living on the site we are designing (and a significant difference for those who design for clients) is the constant osmosis through the skin of the features of the land. Twelve committed land-dwellers may not always see eye to eye, but our bodies tell the same story. That is our Basemap.

After our year of observation, we had the winter of hedgelaying and a summer of harvesting other people's knowledge and experience. We did group dynamic games and consensus workshops. We dowsed and danced, shamanic messages were left in our visitors' book, and we learnt Where Nature Meets Culture. This was a weekend workshop of variety and fun led by lovely people, but my abiding memory is when a local farmer was persuaded to step inside the yurt to help us with a timeline of land-management jobs. To each of the "When do you need to..." questions, his answer remained the same. "When e's ready". From which I learnt another important permaculture principle – Obtain a Yield even if it's not the one you were expecting.

The self-built timber-framed barn catches and stores energy in numerous ways – water, electricity, hay, equipment, etc.

We started with 42 acres of permanent pasture and woodland, with no buildings or water source other than a stream at the bottom of the woods. Deciding where to put our dwellings was a no-brainer – the planning system requires minimal visual impact for development in the open countryside, and who wants to be overlooked on a permanent basis? By some miracle, and a significant feature when deciding to bid for the site, there is one field with high hedges that cannot be looked into from a distance. Despite being on top of a hill and therefore exposed to the elements, this was where we built our benders, yurts and my little wooden roundhouse.

Everything connected

My memory is that the village green concept – dwellings round the field edge with windbreaks in front – was agreed quite easily. It had a logic to it, concentrating human activity in one place, reducing walking distances, a safe place for small children to play, and the windbreak would grow to shield the dwellings from wind and view. We were incorporating the principle of Succession into our design. But Aranya's book told me the question I hadn't remembered, but which Andy Goldring (the Permaculture Association's CEO) had. How much of this 3-acre field should we leave open?

Andy visited us for a week when we got a bit stuck with our design. There is a time when the truism "everything is connected" becomes paralysing. At which point does one cut the chain to make an intervention? To plant the windbreak we needed to decide how big to make the space in the middle. A "Which comes first, the dough or the nut?" conundrum. It was a decision we had put off making because we hadn't worked out how to make it.

Some people weren't bothered about having open space and would happily see trees there, others thought a smallish space for gatherings and ceremonies would suffice, but others had ball games on their mind. It is the only flat area for miles around, with five historic gateways leading into it, and given the name Bowling Green on the old tithe maps. "Obviously" our predecessors had used it for community pastimes, they would have known best, history is to be respected, and anyway where else on site can a chap exercise his human right to play football?

Passion won the principle but still there was the measurement. This was a job for Andy. As Aranya recounts "Andy took them outside and stood them in a circle, posing the question "Is this big enough?" Clearly nobody thought it was, so he gave them each a stick and asked them to walk outwards until they thought it right. After a certain amount of negotiation, the sticks were planted in the ground to define the boundary... ". We learnt from this process and now regularly take our meeting outside to look at the area we are discussing, stand at our boundaries and put sticks in the ground to mark proposed placements.

Like much in permaculture, it seems glaringly obvious once you know. But in the heat and weariness of the moment it can be hard to extract oneself from the melee, define clearly what the problem is, choose the appropriate tool, and get everyone to agree to use it. Another lesson we learnt is not to be afraid to ask for outside facilitation when a mode of group thought or behaviour needs a different approach.

In the Zone

"What's your favourite zone?" is not known to be a hugely successful chat-up line, for reasons I just don't understand. Each zone is adequately well-defined to speak volumes of the person choosing their preference.

Right now, in the middle of a writing 'holiday', a frantically late growing season and all the rest, my favourite zone is Zone 5. Wilderness, area of no human intervention and therefore no work, yippee. Home-makers would go for Zone 0 – the house and immediate surrounds – while more broad-brush temperaments might be happier in Zone 3, with its large-scale potential and comfortable remove from domesticity. I feel a permaculture dating service zoning in.

Zones are about energy efficiency in the Placement of Elements of the design, as well as ensuring enough room for the indigenous plants and animals. They work outwards from a focal point, in our case the field containing our dwellings. Only in books are the zones concentric rings radiating out from this point, but that doesn't matter. The basic principle is that the closer the zone to the focal point, the more energy intensive and productive it will be.

During our year of observation, the big question was "Is this land suited to having a low-impact development on it?" An obvious question perhaps, but sometimes a site's suitability for human projects is overlooked in the excitement of the moment. If you find a stunning piece of land at the right price but it is mostly sloping north, your income-generating plans for a solar 'farm' might have to give way to something more suitable, like skiing.

Equally, the features of the land will often describe the zones for you. Having familiarised ourselves with our beautiful patch, we drew lines on maps and numbered them. We agreed a Zone 5, the non-intervention area, straight away because it was the furthest piece of woodland from our dwellings, it had a secretive quality all of its own, and some interesting old earthworks. An access path runs along the top of it that we walk regularly (to the pub mostly), but otherwise it remains as it has been for decades. Sightings and strange noises confirm "there be beasties" as intended and, in the last week of April, a white carpet of wood anemone.

The other lines we drew have developed wibbles, as the other considerations of Sectors, Microclimates and Beneficial Relationships have been added. But essentially the zones remain the same as we first described. After ten years we are just reaching the outside edge of Zone 1, with still much to do within it. That may sound slow by any standards, but we are not just cultivating the land...

Closing energy loops is a hugely satisfying activity, and having a large site allows much potential for this. We have grazing for animals and space to compost their manure, which goes on vegetable beds, thence to the plate and leftovers back into the compost. This is obviously a diminishing cycle needing further vegetable input, achieved by saving seed for the following year. As well as using manure and garden compost we plant green manures, mulch with scythed hay, and collect nutritious molehills to maintain fertility. Closed cycles are age-old practices abandoned by the 'green revolution' to the detriment of all, but integral to permaculture.

There is nothing quite like being off grid to concentrate the mind on renewable energy sources. We have a mix of pv panels and little wind gennies that electrify our dwellings and communal spaces. These allow us to run lights, computers, music, film and domestic applicances. "Do your panels provide enough electricity?" is a reasonable and frequently asked question. However, the answer comes not in the form of watts and amps, but in what is ample and what is not.

Low-impact wooden roundhouse at Landmatters

Resilience

The permaculture principle of 'each Function is performed by more than one Element, and each element performs more than one function', becomes essential to sustain our human energy, material resources and ultimately the beauty of the land. This is a principle of Resilience and ensures we design in a plan B and maybe C. If one element fails in its function for a period, another can take over that function. But the same element may well continue to perform its other functions. So, for example, the barn roof harvests rainwater, houses lots of solar panels, and provides a dry space underneath for a workshop, hay storage and nesting birds. All these functions are performed elsewhere to a lesser extent, so in an emergency we could get by.

The resilience also comes in terms of not having to stress the land, for example in the event of a crop failure. If a growing area (or a vegetable) that's relied on for protein gets diseased and there is no alternative crop planted elsewhere, the gardener may be tempted to seek a solution in herbicides or pesticides. Having another protein source from a different plant family elsewhere on the plot reduces the pressure to take drastic action and fills the need for protein.

Although this principle encourages 'doubling-up', the multi-functioning of each element means one can use a minimum of 'things' to the maximum benefit. We are able to zone and create intensive, self-sustaining systems that use these inputs efficiently. Concentrating the dwellings, barn, workshops and other structures for human activity in one area is energy efficient. It also means that the rest of the site retains the qualities that drew us here in the first place, and allows its non-human world to continue largely unhindered.

Nitty Gritty

'Low-impact living' slips easily off the tongue, with barely a hint of the enormity of the task. The 'low-impact' bit is relatively easy, and there are plenty of books to tell you what and how. We read them, built our dwellings, made a start on necessary infrastructure, squeezed ourselves through the planning system, grew some food, lured finance into our bank account and volunteer help into our fields, all reused, recycled and as local as possible, except the volunteers who were shiny and new and came from all over. When we were given three years' temporary planning permission we took a deep breath, looked around and realised it was time to address the 'living' bit. In all the frenetic activity of the first few years, the repair and maintenance of personal relationships had slipped repeatedly off the agenda. Peoplecare – one of permaculture's Ethics, alongside Earthcare and Fairshare – was about to take centre stage.

'Community' is about to join 'sustainable' in my dustbin of useless words. Much abused, undefinable, often intangeable, and cyberspace compatible, I find it of limited help as a generic term. Instead, like permaculture itself, it is Site Specific. However, its use is difficult to avoid.

We started by asking what did we want from our community? What would we be prepared to put into it? More bits of paper followed, with workshops, discussions on the nature of trust, respect, autonomy, the personal versus 'public', and the protracted construction of our Holistic Goal aka vision statement – "To embody a deep connection to the web of life, within a thriving community actively creating a sustainable world."

A hardy perennial of community living is the 'relative value of work' discussion. Or maybe it's the discussion that doesn't take place until someone erupts a lavaflow of boiling resentment into someone else's unsuspecting lap.

When you come into the communal bender after a day of compost loo building, cold and thirsty, rain dripping from your nose and hammered thumbs throbbing, it isn't always easy to recognise that the person engrossed in their computer, papers over the table, warm and dry with a cuppa at their elbow, is matching your heroic efforts. A strong dose of legal or financial paperwork can often restore equilibrium, but prevention is always better than cure.

Cue the Way of Council – a facilitated space for heartfelt musings, conflict resolution, deepening relationships, and the expression of emotions that demand to be heard. It is one of the many group processes we tried out and the one that has stuck. It is the place where, for example, parents can express frustration at not feeling valued for their work in raising the children relative, of course, to the work of others. It is where any 'some people aren't pulling their weight' attitudes can be unpicked gently and re-evaluated. Hearing the other side of the story is hugely beneficial in this debate. We come as individuals to this one, trailing our historical baggage of insecurities, hurt, pride and all the rest of our messy selves, and in the process can learn as much about ourselves as each other. Reconstructing concepts of value is a fundamental part of permaculture and a fertile Edge to tread.

We return to this theme from time to time, but mostly so we can design in solutions. With less pressure on the group now and more experience we have come to appreciate the different skills we bring, the jobs that need to rotate because they are a pain, and how over time things tend to balance out. Most important is the recognition that we all benefit from the work of each other on a daily basis.

What we didn't do much of was to talk politics or discuss world affairs, with their natural follow-on to personal values, beliefs and principles. We have no group creed to buy into, or single goal to achieve. Each of us has our own ambition for the project, and our own integration of 'project' with 'living'.

Permaculture serves to help us accommodate these differences and we've made use of many of its tools. One that illustrates the project/life conundrum is when a question is asked like "Do we need to produce more food?" and people place themselves in a line between two points according to their strength of agreement. As we shuffle into position, someone invariably asks "Do you mean that I agree to produce more food, or that someone should?" Is it what Landmatters needs or what the individual wants to do? In co-operative terms, it might be a sign of success when this question is no longer asked, when the personal and collective good are perceived as the same. But is that degree of cohesion either desirable or necessary to achieve a thriving community? People tend to answer by their actions.

It is also worth considering the myriad issues at play when we find it easier to come together immediately when the farmer's sheep escape than to turn up for a prearranged work day on a fellow member's garden or house. In practice, on the occasions when the parallel lines of personal and Co-op converge, the sense of community is tangible and joyful.

Those moments are to be celebrated, but the unremarkable ones should not be ignored, revealing as they do the incremental building of community. What has now become embedded into life at Landmatters was once a conscious, consensus decision.

A visitor recently congratulated us on our car-sharing policy. Not many groups do this apparently, whereas I would assume that they did because it seems an obvious thing to do. But when Mr Ford planned the internal combustion engine revolution that has ruled our lives for decades he didn't want us to divorce ourselves from private car ownership, arrange journeys around others' lives, return vehicles on time (not just disappearing off to the beach because we felt like it)!

The lending of tools (trust) and returning them in good order (respect) can be a wonderfully contentious facet of community life. Communal meals, meeting structures and times, domestic funds and tasks have all evolved according to a rolling process of Evaluation of the needs of the people involved. Forming community around shared ideas and ideals is fine, but on its own can easily unravel. As people have found throughout history, it is actions that count. The expressions of empathy, care of the sick, a sympathetic ear, working together or just a helping hand at the right time all create a sense of belonging.

As the project has evolved, community-building has become more organic than contrived, based on practical co-operation. The goat group, car-sharing, gardening partnerships, celebrations, children playing and being looked after together, local and mutual friends, and of course cooking and eating together – all weave a web of mutual aid and personal connection between us.

Livelihoods
Creating a livelihood from the land is a requirement of our planning permission as well as a basic tenet of a land-based permaculture project. Starting out it is sensible to design for future uncertainties. Will people stay and build the business they are suggest-

ing? Is there a market for the product? Having lots of small enterprises seemed the way to go, each person or small groupmaking a modest income from their chosen activity without jeopardising the security of the whole. Financial Resilience was the aim.

After a few years we evaluated the efficiency of this approach. It wasn't a complex procedure – very little was happening! The site is large, the project ambitious, and we needed infrastructure in order to live and work. Generous grants and donations meant we had the funds to build a barn, a yurt, compost loos, communal bender and raised beds, buy compost and seeds, repair fences, drill a borehole, appeal the initial refusal of planning permission, make car parking for visitors, and buy essential equipment. This took all our time and energy.

But it became apparent that most of the income we were generating was coming from a salad growing business and our educational activities. We decided to 'rationalise' and concentrate on education and horticulture.

An area north of the barn had been chosen as the commercial growing area, and a design has gradually been implemented over a number of years. First there were raised beds for the mixed salad leaves, then came strawberries for an early, high-income crop, followed by raspberries and blueberries. In the meantime a second area was covered in horticultural plastic so it would be clear of grass when needed. This year it became the site of The Polypod – our luscious wooden polytunnel.

The Limiting Factors of our design for this commercial growing area – space and labour – led to an adaptation of the alley cropping model along with some forest garden ideas. Alley cropping (the growing of veg and/ or grains between rows of often nitrogen-fixing trees or bushes) is gaining popularity as the ecological benefits are better documented. So in the area between the salad beds and the strawberries we dug bendy paths that created raised islands of soil. On each is planted an edible bush – black and red currants, gooseberries, goji berries – undersown with groundcover plants including chicory and Siberian claytonia. Running down the middle are four fruit trees.

The fruit from these will increase our products for sale, the trees will eventually cast shade on the salad crops to reduce bolting in high summer, the edible groundcover adds variety to the winter salad mix, and

Innovative wood-framed polypod designed by a local craftsman using local timber and Landmatters' oak

the whole area will be a veritable feast for pollinating insects. That's the plan anyway.

Part of our planning permission specifies research into and demonstrating permaculture principles and techniques. As this growing area is worked intensively we can make regular observations of how nature responds to this novel arrangement and share them with others.

Our other main income stream is environmental education. From the very beginning we were getting interest from schools and colleges wanting to understand what we were doing and how. Since we started, the Transition Town movement has taken off and we regularly host visits from TT groups from around the country and abroad. Local schools visit for a day of nature-based activities and a taste of low-impact living, young students making that transition from "Aren't you bored without a telly" to "Mum, I'm not coming home, I'm going to live in a yurt". Some groups we teach and others use the land as a venue to develop their own curriculum work.

Most of our education work has evolved through a mixture of personal contacts, networks, people's involvement in other activities, and our website. We also do a 'guided tour' on the second Saturday of each month for those who just want to have a look around.

As well as earning us some wages the education business pays for the running costs of the Co-op. It therefore demonstrates a classic permaculture model of an element that requires a lot of input at the beginning (infrastructure, learning and experience) but once established needs far less input to achieve ever-increasing outputs, in the form of money, permaculture Dissemination, and a rich experience for students and teachers.

Occasionally new members join us, bringing the richness of their lives, enthusiastic energy, and skills that make the unfeasible seem a real possibility. Each year I deepen my connection with our patch of land, as my peripheral vision registers the incidental changes and my body clock surrenders to the changing seasons. Each day I know how lucky I am.

I've tried to illustrate how permaculture is Landmatters' framework for low-impact living. It takes discipline and honesty of thought and action, often becoming more difficult in the details. But it's an approach that encourages us to be versatile, flexible, inclusive, democratic and creative. It can cope with conflict, large groups and small, and Invisible Structures like networks and how to arrange the finances.

Struggle as we do with a never-ending list of jobs to complete, our own flawed personalities, and a world that can appear to be moving rapidly towards its terminal unravelling, it does seem that we are 'doing permaculture'. Passing on the concepts and practicalities that have got caught in our collective web is an act of celebration, and we welcome anyone with an interest in what we do – including those wanting to set up their own permaculture plot and need to ask "Do you have any tips on how to design with a large group of people?".

"For action is the life of all, and if thou doest not act, thou doest nothing."
Gerrard Winstanley, 1649

Charlotte Oliver
is a founder member of Landmatters Permaculture Community in Devon and scything enthusiast.

All you need is a Tipi?

RICK MAYES

Diggers & Dreamers editor Jonathan How asks Rick Mayes from Tipi Valley some essential questions about this 40-year-old experiment in reconnecting with nature

JH What were the origins of Tipi Valley, what is its founding myth?

RM Well, briefly, the wave of euphoria created when the hippie Summer of Love burst out in 1967 created a large number of urban alternative types and spawned a new culture, who tended to wear their hair long etc, and believe in such slogans as "Make Love Not War", and "All you need is Love", and maybe with a new ecological awareness inspired by such sayings as "The Earth does not belong to us, we belong to the Earth". Inspired too by the first amazing photographs of planet Earth taken from outer space by the Apollo 11 moon mission in 1969 – for the first time we could see this huge and wonderful orb spinning through the skies. So beautiful. So alive. So strong. So vulnerable. That image of planet Earth became a

Tipi circle with the Big Lodge, years and years ago

powerful icon of the environmental movement that it certainly helped inspire. Greenpeace, Friends of the Earth and other environmental groups soon started to spring up, to campaign, to try to save the planet and its creatures from human devastation and deforestation.

Hippies communicated with each other via a lively underground press and with the free festivals movement, which really took off in Britain in about 1969, the year of the legendary Woodstock Festival in the USA.

For our part of the story, it is the three Windsor People's Free Festivals held in Windsor Great Park from 1972 to 1974 that are important, the last one being violently broken up by police.

In 1974 the whole feeling of the festival was that of being in the vanguard of a new age, a new civilisation being born, based on love and peace and sharing, a new way of living... if only we had a faintest clue as to how we should do it. Chris Wait was there with his family living in his stunning new white tipi. He'd seen the design in The Last Whole Earth Catalog and had paid a sailmaker to make him one. A tipi! This was a eureka moment for us! The tipi: light, portable, relatively cheap and gentle on the Earth: yes, we could actually live in tipis!

So that winter of 1974 a small gathering of people who had met through these free festivals started a little tipi village over in Wales, at a farm at Cwmann near Lampeter, at the invitation of Andrew Cripps, grandson of the former cabinet minister. There were only a dozen people to start with, but it slowly grew to being a couple of dozen with a tipi circle of about eight tipis, with a large communal one at the centre, called the Big Lodge where tribal get-togethers happened and where visitors could stay, and the Big Lodge is a tradition which continues to this day in Tipi Valley. They stayed there 18 months and needed to find somewhere else to move on to.

Tipi circle in 1998

Rik's Lodge in the snow

Word had reached the hippies at Cwmann that land was for sale up the Cwmdu valley near Talley. So various hippies went over there and found old Captain Blount, a rebellious old farmer who disliked authority, living in his chosen squalor at Pistyll Gwyn. He was prepared to sell off his poor wet north-facing lands, field by field, to any hippy who wanted to pay him. And payment was on easy terms too, after moving onto the land most people would go up and pay their £5 or £10 weekly to old Nab, as he was called, and get a receipt.

So, in that long hot summer of 1976 Tipi Valley was born, with a tipi circle of seven or eight tipis and in the next three years that number grew to 18.

JH What were the locals' reactions then, and what are they now?

RM Right from the beginning, though there was a strong tribal feeling, the settlement was strongly anarchistic, so it took us a few years to sort out the problems with neighbouring farmers. The worst was the dog problem, dogs killing sheep. By 1984 we had to ban keeping dogs, they were a real problem within our village as well as with the farmers.

That was all a long time ago. Those same farmers, now old men, are now good friends of the community, and stayed true to what they said on TV in 1984, "We don't mind how they live now, we just don't want them to go stealing firewood and letting their dogs kill sheep".

These days the people of Tipi Valley are vital to the common wealth of the local community, the children go to the local Welsh-speaking primary school, so they all learn to speak Welsh. The local community is proud of Tipi Valley, and this is immortalised in the tapestry hanging in the local church showing Tipi Valley as one of the notable places in the parish. Actually, we are also proud to be such a part of our tiny local village of Cwmdu, with its quaint old post office, shop and tavern and chapel, all owned by the National Trust and run by local community volunteers, and the wonderful welcome you always find there.

JH Tell us how the landscape of the valley has changed in the last 40 years.

RM When we started living on the land, it had been decimated by the overgrazing of sheep, ever since the indigenous subsistence farmers had to abandon the old ways in the 1920's, and move into neighbouring villages. Not a single new tree had been able to establish itself since that time. What we managed to do was to put a fence around all the land we owned in the village, even in those days it must have been the best part of a mile long. Far more impressive than any tree planting we have done is the response of Mother Nature, it is wonderful how the trees so quickly regenerate and create what they want to be, a temperate rain forest, and the wildflowers and the fauna with them, giving us an environment which is 100% nature to be part of, it is what inspires our beliefs and spirituality.

Thatched hut

JH How is the major part of the land owned?

RM Unfortunately, the evolution of Tipi Valley does not provide a blueprint that it is easy to follow, because we had the rare good fortune of finding two neighbouring farmers who would sell us land, field by field, whenever we had saved up to buy a bit more. For the first three years it was individuals buying their own bit. In 1979 we formed the Land Fund to collect money to buy the land in common. One thing living in a mobile structure like a tipi taught us, is that if we share the land together, each of us has a hugely greater choice of where to live, than if we confined ourselves to our own private muddy acre.

Every time we make a purchase of land, that land becomes a trust with four trustees.

So now we have over a dozen of these trusts, each with its own trustees, each with its own name, but known by the collective name of The Tipis Trust. About 100 acres. And there's also about another 100 acres around the valley privately owned, so that Tipi

Roof frame for turf-roofed roundhouse

Valley itself is about 200 acres, and the perimeter fence runs for more than 3 miles.

JH Are there any legal structures at all?

RM We don't really need a courthouse or prison. A set of stocks on the village green could be useful sometimes! (question answered more seriously below)

JH How is it decided who can live in Tipi Valley?

RM Tipi Valley has always been an open community, and the people put money into the Land Fund to make it possible for other people to live on the land, as beneficiaries of the Trust, not for it to become a private estate.

So Tipi Valley is in principle an open community. Theoretically anyone with a tipi or yurt can come and give it a go, though some villagers would prefer visitors to stay in the Big Lodge for a while first, so that we can get to know each other. People who are not suited to this way of life, or who just don't get on with their neighbours, they soon leave. You really have to love this way of life to be able to cope with the Welsh climate. So it is self-selecting really, we don't need a committee.

JH Is there anything that people formally join when they move in?

RM Tipi Valley is not an organisation or club or legal entity, or even a commune. It is a village, and we never charge ourselves rent, and we never charge anything to visitors. You have to make your own living. Our common bank account is for the Land Fund, and we're still saving. We gather for celebration whenever we can, but we don't often have formal meetings unless we need one. To sort matters out we chat amongst ourselves, a village project will usually be led by the persons best skilled for it. The village is like a large family, and with three generations living here now, though we have no chiefs, elders are respected for their knowledge, experience, and possibly, their wisdom.

But to answer your question, it could be helpful if you joined the Electoral Roll.

Turf-roofed roundhouse

JH Tell us more about the Big Lodge.

RM The Big Lodge is the very large tipi at the heart of Tipi Valley, which has always been an essential feature of our culture. It is there that we have many of our feasts, music making and gatherings.

The Big Lodge is very basic. Large tipi, rushes covering the floor, large hearth in the middle of the tipi. Two big smoke flap poles outside that need to be adjusted according to the wind direction. We bring our own sheepskins to sit on, shoes off at the door.

Visitors are welcome to stay in the Big Lodge, for any length of time they like.

They must survive for themselves, providing their own food, finding their own firewood, cooking over the central fire, fetching water from the well, and what we ask of them in return is to keep the Big

Turf-roofed roundhouse

Lodge looked after and tidy. Which is work enough for the visitor, we don't ask for more.

Being so large, the Big Lodge is harder to live in than our own cosy little homes, so it is a good survival experience to stay in there, and villagers will notice how much effort is put in by a visitor to keep the Big Lodge a clean, tidy, welcoming space, with maybe some fresh rushes on the floor. It's more fun when there's other guests to share with, and much more fun if the weather is dry and sunny than if it's wet and drippy.

JH What is it that draws people here more than anything else?

RM Well, there's this brilliant website called www.diggersanddreamers.org.uk! I get lots of emails, via the D&D website, asking to visit. Nearly all of them express a great longing to escape somehow from the destructive nature-excluding civilisation we have had built for ourselves, and to do something real with their lives and work time, to find somewhere nourishing to bring up their children, and to be more in harmony with nature, and to find happiness.

JH Do you think that Tipi Valley is a vision of how we'll all be living in the future?

RM No, in the future the human race will be stuck in a fleet of spaceships drifting optimistically through space, looking for a new planet to replace the one we'd finished with.

Meanwhile, I see Tipi Valley as an encouragement to people, so that when they look aghast at the destruction our civilisation is wreaking upon the Earth, including their own personal carbon footprints, they can say "but it doesn't have to be like this" and know that something different is possible. But to find the opportunity is so difficult.

A visit here can be inspiring, because these days we're not only living in tipis and yurts, but there are also now about a dozen turf-roofed roundhouses, with straw bale and daub walls. They are stunningly beautiful, built with very inexpensive locally sourced materials, very heat efficient and easy to live in. But not very easy to get planning permission for. It would be good if there were other villages like ours in Britain. If our civilisation collapses and people are forced to live very much more simply and have to struggle to survive off the land, the communities emerging are more likely to be shanty towns than picturesque hippy villages. So is Tipi Valley a vision of how we'll all be living in the future? Maybe a hint, a glimpse of the vision that it could be possible for modern humans to be living in paradise on planet Earth.

The Big Lodge

Rev Rik Mayes
is an ordained Anglican and Earth-Centred Minister serving the Hippie Community in Wales from his tipi in Tipi Valley. He is also available to conduct occasional church services in the locality.

Escape to the Future:

LIZ LAINÉ

*Hockerton Housing Project has been a flagship of sustainable energy
since the 1990s... but it's also good at social sustainability*

Here at Hockerton Housing Project our aim is to 'bring sustainability to life' by showing that low environmental impact can be delivered at low cost, and with huge social benefits. Too often the media frame eco homes as glass-walled and gadget-driven, putting the dream out of reach for most of us due to the dual restrictions of cost and the planning system. Our approach is achievable now, with a build cost comparable to new homes but with far greater environmental, social and economic benefits than delivered by any standard or regulation.

An overview
Hockerton Housing Project is an earth-sheltered co-housing development of five homes that seeks to 'bring sustainability to life'. We own our homes and also have private gardens, but then share time, skills and resources to generate electricity equivalent to our use from the wind and sun, we harvest and treat our own water, and recycle waste to limit the emission of greenhouse gases. We also grow much of our own fruit and vegetables, rear sheep and chickens for meat and eggs, and keep bees.

After a lengthy planning phase, the construction of the self-build project started in August 1996 and the residents finally moved in between February and September 1998. The residents meet three

© *Hockerton Housing Project*

times a month to manage the project, overseeing the management of the land and shared services, and the related trading company, This delivers a range of services to support self-builders, developers, planners and academia including onsite tours and consultancy services for sustainable housing, water systems and community energy. So far 20,000 people have visited to see sustainability in action, we have had media coverage from across the world including New Zealand and South Korea, and closer to home we helped deliver one of the first community-owned wind turbines in the country for the village of Hockerton.

Governance
The planning phase was a challenging time for the self-builders but it delivered two documents that remain the cornerstones for the community:

Background document
This 'visionary' document enshrines the foundation of the project, laying out its aims and objectives. Much of the subsequent development of the project stems from the core principles set out here

Land management plan
This defines how the land must be developed in a sustainable way.

These visions have then been operationalised by the Primary Rules of the co-operative constitutions. These bring together the requirements set out in the planning agreements (section 106), and lease agreements. These documents are legally binding, but the Project also has a number of Secondary Rules that evolve according to circumstance and cover more practical issues such as pay-rates.

The rules are rarely referred to as they are generally common sense to those who understand sustainable living, but they can be used to prevent future misunderstandings and allow all community members a say in how the group should operate.

All this is summarised by our mission to 'bring sustainability to life'. We can't force sustainable choices on people, but what we can provide is a living example of sustainable living that offers (contrary to the media stereotype) more comfort and less cost.

Living sustainably

So what is really like to live in a home that comes with environmental and social 'rules'? Are the rules 'just a piece of paper' or too much bureaucracy?

We are happy to say that we certainly don't have the latter, but residents continue to have a very active role in keeping environmental, social and economic sustainability in balance and at the heart of the Project, and make the rules a living guide to their activities.

Environmental sustainability

There are three principle ways in which we try to minimise our impact on the environment

- Energy and water efficient community

- Food-growing

- Land management

The homes at Hockerton Housing Project are designed in such a way that no central heating system is necessary. The use of high thermal mass, passive solar gain and super-insulation means that the warmth of the sun is captured in the fabric of the house through the year to keep it cool in summer and warm in winter. By only needing energy for appliances, ventilation and water heating, and reducing hot water demand through our super-insulated 'Hotsi' water tanks and efficient water use, residents have energy bills one-sixth of the national average.

Visitors will often comment first on the way the homes are earth-sheltered. The earth-sheltering is not necessary for insulation, and the design decision was driven more by environmental aesthetics and biodiversity objectives than the need for energy efficiency. The large windows to the south mean that light streams in and north-facing windows are not missed. The key energy efficiency features are hidden in the fabric of the homes, but that is easy to forget when living in one of them.

It is the simplicity of this approach that is both Hockerton Housing Project's greatest strength and greatest weakness. There is little commercial gain to be had from building such houses: no patents, no gadgets that need ongoing maintenance, any construction firm could build them, and they deliver greatly reduced energy bills. However, for these reasons together with

© *Hockerton Housing Project*

the fantastic comfort levels in summer and winter, we wonder why anyone would go any other route as a self-builder!

Having reduced our energy consumption, we are then able to cost-effectively generate the energy we do use from renewable sources. The five homes on the Project share two wind turbines (total 11 kW) and two solar PV arrays (total 13.6 kW), and share the benefits of lower cost energy and income from exported energy. Whilst the first of the wind turbines attracted strong opposition locally, its eventual installation broke down barriers. The second wind turbine went unopposed, in 2009 we project managed the installation of a 225kW wind turbine on the ridge above the village, and wind turbines are being installed by a high proportion of local farmers. Pioneers are vital in the environmental movement as so many barriers need to be broken down. And behind every direct action that captures the media's attention through shock tactics there must be a balancing story that demonstrates that the change being sought is desirable, attainable and affordable. That is why we continue to tell the story of our homes and various energy and water systems through the media and by opening our doors to visitors from the UK and beyond.

Reducing our impact on the environment from the food we eat also has a positive impact on the quality of life and, if anything, adds to it. The food is fresher than that bought from the supermarket, only we spend more time on the vegetable patch and less in the supermarket. The sweetcorn eaten off the cob thirty minutes after harvesting does taste dramatically different. Sweetcorn grown many miles away, transported over large distances, stored in depots, and stacked on shelves for days cannot have the same nutrient and health value. By growing much of our own food using organic methods we can enjoy better quality food, whilst avoiding the energy and pollution associated with delivering food to our plates.

We estimate that we grow between 50 and 70% of our own fruit and vegetables; we also have hens to supply eggs and keep a small flock of sheep to assist with land management and for meat. The sheep's role in land management is to keep the grass grazed, and a very important role it is, given the size of the site.

Hockerton Housing Project leases about half of the 25 acres governed by a land management plan agreed

© Hockerton Housing Project

between the landowners and the local authority. We have two leases in place, one long lease (originally 999 years) that covers the land on which the homes and amenities sit, and a farm tenancy for additional land. This additional land allows us more space to grow food, it is not necessary for us to meet our objectives but it suits both parties at present. The leases and related documents are the one area that are most at risk of criticisms of complexity and bureaucracy, hence the development of the overarching plain language Rules.

Other than keeping the grass down, land management activity covers a range of activity relating to woodland, planting and the wildlife pond. The objectives are a mix of maintenance and the promotion of biodiversity.

Different elements of the related work appeal to different people, and there are economies of scale to be had from sharing the workload involved. The framework for this is set out in the Background document, and in our Rules. Each house is required to spend 300 hours on 'organics', which incorporates vegetable-growing, animal husbandry and land management. Hours are recorded on a monthly basis to ensure everyone keeps up-to-date, though some of us are often found out pruning or cleaning out the chickens on New Years Eve to make up those last few hours!

Social sustainability

I've subconsciously chosen to write this in the first-person-plural. Never mind what my English teachers would think about not making that a conscious decision: how can I write on behalf of my neighbours? I certainly couldn't imagine it during my time in London, when the only time my husband and I met the immediate neighbours was during fire alarms.

The formal difference here is again in our Rules. We all know what we have signed up for, but more important in my view are our shared values. Moving up from London we could not predict how the co-operative nature of the development would work for us, but what we did know was that this was a group of people who shared our values and were 'doers'. In our view (then and now) if you not only agree on where you are trying to get to, but also are willing to do something about it, then you're going to get on!

You may not always agree on the details of how something is done, but this rarely causes problems for three reasons. Firstly the mix of skills at Hockerton Housing Project is such that there tends only to be one or two 'experts' in any field. We test each other on decisions but there are rarely strongly contradictory views, and we expect each other to listen and incorporate views. Secondly, time is precious and if someone is willing to take an idea forward, it is difficult to make the case for a different approach if you cannot contribute yourself. Thirdly, with only five houses we have a cohesive team, with high levels of interconnectivity and no need for sub-groups. The relatively small number of homes means no factions emerge and a balance is found across activities, with members leading activities in one area and assisting in others. I believe that it is due to this balance of skills, time and leadership that, in my time here at least, we have never had to resort to a formal decision-making process.

So what do we 'do' to deliver social sustainability? The formal aspect of this is actually rather informal. Two or three times a month we meet on a Friday night to take a look at what's going on at the Project, whether that relates to food-growing, land management, energy and water systems or our shared business. It's a great way to ensure jobs are assigned and a record kept of our achievements, but social sustainability comes not only from meeting up and talking with others. Social sustainability comes from broader wellbeing.

According to the New Economics Foundation, 'high levels of well-being mean that we are more able to respond to difficult circumstances, to innovate and constructively engage with other people and the world around us'. We think that at Hockerton Housing Project the combination of the private homes, shared land and co-operative business promote wellbeing in a variety of complementary ways:

- Responsibility: each adult has responsibility to support shared elements of the project, giving them a strong sense of self within the community

- Community: alongside that sense of self there is also a strong sense of support

- Physical exercise: every family helps grow food and maintain the land

- Mental stimulation: residents take responsibility for actions

- Fulfilment: new skills and friendships develop as a result

So after all this mental stimulation and physical work, what do we do in our spare time? You might see us playing volleyball with our neighbours on a summer-evening, barbecuing a carp from the lake, watching water-voles in the lake from a conservatory, chasing ducks out of the garden, or dining outside looking over the lake. And the year is punctuated with social events such as a shared birthday meal, the Easter egg hunt, trick or treating, and Santa's annual visit to our Christmas party.

Of course the kids are the real beneficiaries; making dens and fires, swinging over the stream, sailing, canoeing and swimming in the lake, forming gangs and making plays and shows to entertain the weary adults after a day on the land or in the office. On the other hand you may find us inside watching a DVD or catching up with the wider world through social networking, but of course with gadgets powered by the wind and sun.

Fifteen years in and three of the homes have now changed hands, with average tenure similar to the national average of twelve years. Like any change in membership of a close-knit team there is an impact on others, but whilst old hands are missed, new residents are welcomed for their new skills, ideas and enthusiasm.

Economic sustainability

The Hockerton Housing Project isn't about self-sacrifice or *The Good Life*; it's about creating a good quality lifestyle without having a negative impact on the environment. But does it pay to live sustainably?

© *Hockerton Housing Project*

Within the Project there was originally an intention of having an internal system of credits, along the LETS model. Over time, the reality was that no credit system was needed other than a record of hours worked as everyone's time has the same value. In summary, and explored further below, each household is required to contribute 600 hours per year to the Project. This is roughly divided between agricultural work (300 hours), commercial work (300 hours) and facilities management (2-4 hours per week or capital contributions).

This is a significant contribution and is meant to be – the planning authorities wanted a legacy that ensured residents made a real commitment to the Project and to the land. The upside is that all these activities have an economic benefit, through savings or income.

The economic benefit of the work we put into the Project comes in three forms. Each home's 300 hours on the land saves them money on fruit, vegetables, eggs and meat. Some would say it also saves money on gym fees!

The residents also try to share out work that helps maintain key facilities such as the road, and the renewable energy and water harvesting and treatment systems. There is no minimum time commitment as work is only undertaken as and when it's needed, with some maintenance jobs carried out quarterly. We give this work a monetary value, to recognise that time spent on facilities management saves money on energy and water bills, but by sharing the work out we avoid significant outlay and benefit from each others' time and skills.

The third form of economic benefit is the most traditional as we run a trading company to deliver a range of services to the outside world. Originally envisaged as an agricultural business, the trading company quickly adapted to the demand to see sustainability in action. At first the residents had to work out how to manage those people who literally turned up at the gates wanting to look around. From that start we now run a range of tours, events and consultancy services that take people from an introduction to sustainable living, provide support through planning applications through to design work for self-builders and developers. We also use our experience with micro and medium-sized community renewable energy projects to help others, again through training days or consultancy services.

The governance of the trading company mirrors that of the Project, except that it allows for members who are non-resident. It is a fully democratic co-operative, with all members paid the same net hourly rate of pay whatever the task or responsibilities. The only requirement on members is that we work a minimum number of hours. There is then an unwritten and informal shared responsibility to maintain and develop the business, making best use of the skills within the group at the time. Whilst everyone has some skills that hold a higher value in the outside world, the fact that we are all working on projects we want to do alongside tasks that are necessary but mundane (with a lower pay rate in the outside world), means that the right balance is found both in pay and job satisfaction.

None of this is profit-making, but it does pay a basic salary and allows us to invest in the future of the Project, whether that is building a visitor centre or installing new renewable energy systems, or maximise the reach of our message through some cross-subsidisation of services.

What does the future hold?

The future looks positive for the Project. The durability of the homes and the Rules that govern the Project mean the basics will stay in place for decades, even centuries to come. Residents will save more money on their energy and water bills as prices rise. A medium-term plan to go off-grid would protect us from brown-outs. Our exposure to the risks of climate change are mitigated by the homes' capacity to stay cool and the water management systems around the site. And the business can continue to adapt to the skills and wishes of the current residents.

But life at the Project is not just about renewable energy or the way the homes look. It is a feeling of escape to the future, but not the future so often envisaged by the media. We like our technology, but are not bound by the latest fads; instead our escape to the future is one where self-sufficiency and a healthy, biodiverse environment generate a sense of wellbeing. Sadly we are yet to see many other co-housing projects duplicate the achievement of delivering such high environmental performance whilst also engendering strong social cohesion and economic stability. And that is what we would like the future to hold.

Liz Lainé
is a director of Hockerton Housing Project and a consumer policy advocate specialising in sustainable consumption and the low carbon transition. Her current focus is on the development of the Green Deal and the UK's micro generation strategy.

Tinkers' Bubble

PETER 'PEDRO' BRACE

Celebrating its 20th Anniversary... we catch up with this remarkable and iconic Somerset community

Tinkers' Bubble is a low impact woodland community in Somerset, with a passion for sustainability and for working the land. It was founded in 1994 on a 40 acre site, of which 27 acres is woodland. Currently there are ten adults and two children resident in the community.

We don't allow the use of fossil fuels within our land, other than a few minor exceptions, such as the occasional use of paraffin lamps. Our homes are built using timber grown on site, plus recycled materials. We grow much of our own food and we strive to be as sustainable as possible.

We try to earn as much of our living as possible from the land, primarily through our apple juice, forestry and education businesses, but also through other smaller projects, such as furniture making.

We are not connected to the National Grid and a small array of solar panels provides our minimal electricity needs.

History
The community was initially established by a group of friends involved in the M3 Twyford Down road protest and other similar protests in the early 1990s. The friends had all been looking for a piece of land

to rent or buy, when it was discovered that the owner of Norton Covert, (the area of woodland and orchard now know as Tinkers' Bubble) was willing to sell.

The 40 acre site comprised 15 acres of Douglas fir plantation, mostly on fairly steep terrain; 4 acres of Douglas fir planted amongst mixed deciduous trees; 5 acres of larch, much of it leaning and suffering from butt rot; 14 acres of apple orchards and two acres of mixed deciduous trees, but swamped with laurel. Most of the land is situated on south facing slopes and it contains a spring, which was known as Tinkers' Bubble, and from which the community took its name.

Thatched communal building

Norton Covert was ideal in many respects, but was larger than any of the friends had been considering and certainly beyond their individual means. The group therefore decided to purchase the land co-operatively, with one individual investing a significant proportion of the total cost.

The land is held by a co-operative of shareholders; some are residents, others are former residents and a few are individuals who invested in the project, but chose not to reside. There are thirty shares and currently there are seventeen shareholders, of whom six are residents. Some shareholders have several shares and the community has collectively purchased the remainder. Any residents who are not shareholders would be expected to buy in after a year or so. Payment for shares can be made on a weekly basis, as the residents earn money from our activities.

The group moved onto the land on 1 January 1994 and started building simple homes without applying for planning permission. It wasn't long before local residents complained to the local authority, fearing the worst.

One of the Tinkers' Bubble residents at the time, Simon Fairlie, fought the planning system for five years, finally attaining five years temporary planning permission in 1999. The initial planning permission was refused, but was granted on appeal. This decision was called in by the Department of the Environment and overturned by the Secretary, John Gummer. We therefore appealed against this decision in the High Court and lost. Permission was finally granted only after another application was submitted. In the meantime the national government had changed from Conservative to Labour.

One of the key arguments in our planning application was a functional need to live on the land we are working. We need to milk our cows twice a day. Polytunnels covering vegetables need opening and closing, to protect the crops from overheating or getting too cold. Slugs need to be removed at night. Equipment needs to be protected from theft by our presence. Seedlings need to be protected from frosts. These arguments and others support our need to live on the land.

Since then, a further ten years' temporary planning permission was granted in 2004 and the community is preparing for the next application in 2014. The majority of the local residents seem to have accepted Tinkers' Bubble; many of their fears have proved unfounded, the community has become more established and recently we have been working to demonstrate the positive work we are doing here.

At times we have had difficulty with communicating with the local community, as this is very dependent on one or two of our members taking the initiative. And it requires time, which could otherwise be spent on one of the many tasks requiring attention. Recently, we started holding an annual open day to show people in the area what we have achieved and what we plan to do. In the past we have grown vegetables to sell at local markets, which is a great way to keep in touch with the local community. Currently we are concentrating on growing more food for ourselves, but in the future we hope to grow enough surplus food to sell.

Food

We grow most of our fruit and vegetables and we have cows for milk, yoghurt and cheese. We don't tend to eat much meat, but we get occasional road kill. We also hunt and eat grey squirrels and wood pigeons, which are both pests. Whilst some members of the community don't eat meat, others feel it is better to eat meat than to buy in the equivalent vegan alternatives, which are produced, packaged and transported using fossil fuels. The majority of our bought-in food is purchased from an ethical wholesaler and we do not buy any communal food from supermarkets. We mostly buy in grains and pulses and some treats such as coffee, sugar and spices. Wherever possible, we buy organic food.

We have two short-legged Dexter cows and their two calves. They graze our orchards. This reduces the work required to maintain the orchards, converting the grass into milk and beef. This breed of cow is very small, which means they can easily graze under the trees and they require much less food than commercial varieties. They are also very hardy and eat many of the weeds, which we would otherwise have to scythe. Our working horses also graze the orchards, effectively converting the grass into physical work.

We also keep a few chickens for eggs and bees for honey. The chickens eat all of our scraps, but we do still have to buy in feed. We currently have two colonies of bees and intend to increase this number significantly. There is no organic sugar grown commercially in this country and the production of sugar from sugar beet is a very intensive industrial process. Imported sugar requires vast quantities of water and is responsible for displacing millions of peasants around the world. Like other imports, it also requires unsustainable shipping.

We are therefore very keen to eliminate our dependence on sugar. As well as harvesting honey, we have started experimenting with growing sugar beet and using it in its raw state. We have also reduced our dependency by bottling fruit rather than making jam.

Outdoor washing up area

Communal life

We live very communally, more so than many other communities. The fire-pit is the heart of the community, where we often have breakfast or lunch together and we eat together every night, taking turns to cook. This is a very important aspect of our community, as it brings us all together every night, and also conserves wood and our time.

It does require a day to prepare the meal. Cutting firewood, stoking fires and heating water on the fires take a surprising amount of time, but coming home to a hot meal is something for the rest to look forward to at the end of a hard day's work.

Most decisions are made formally by consensus at monthly meetings, where we always try to reach a compromise. We often discuss more contentious issues beforehand through private chats. Many issues are discussed informally over communal dinner. If people opt out of sharing meals, the community loses the opportunity to have these discussions, which we believe significantly reduce conflict in formal meetings.

Every fortnight we have a communal work-week, and residents are expected to spend at least three days working on communal projects. This week is often started with a short meeting to discuss what communal work needs to be done and to arrange days to work together on specific projects.

Communal living facilitates sharing family responsibilities, which gives parents more freedom in work and leisure. We enjoy the majority of the work we do so much that we find little time for leisure, but we do like to get out from time to time. We don't watch television, but rarely find ourselves short of entertainment. Socialising with volunteers, music and crafts take up much of our free time in the evenings.

Transportation
We do have one car between us, which we run on used chip fat bio-diesel when we can get hold of it. Unfortunately this is becoming increasingly difficult. We avoid using the car for the majority of journeys, preferring to cycle or walk. We have two tandems, which enables us to pick people up, or drop them off.

Woodland management
One of the important elements of the community is management of the woodlands and the ability to process the harvested timber. We have taken advice from the Forestry Commission on how to manage the woodland sustainably and have been thinning the Douglas fir trees, to provide enough space for the remaining trees to mature. These trees are still relatively young and closely planted, so no replanting is required in these areas. Elsewhere, we have cleared small areas of the larch, replacing it with ash, sweet chestnut and cherry. In order to process the felled timber we have access to a traditional sawmill on the site. This comprises an antique saw bench and portable steam engine, currently housed in a temporary barn for sound insulation purposes.

Steam engine to power sawmill

The larch was planted amongst coppiced hazel stools, which were abandoned after the conifers were planted. Over the last 13 years, the remaining stools have been restored and now provide a substantial proportion of our firewood. When this work began, some members of the community felt that we should relax our fossil fuel policy and use chain saws to tackle the tougher stools, but the community stuck to its principles and organised coppicing weekends for volunteers, which have turned out to be very popular, proving once again that we can manage the land without fossil fuels.

In other areas, the majority of the laurel has been removed and we have started removing diseased trees.

Infrastructure

There was no infrastructure to start with and in the early days the community had to rapidly build houses, a kitchen, fences to keep livestock in or pests out, irrigation and field shelters. Gardens had to be freshly dug and many new skills learned.

In the beginning, water had to be carried up the hill from the spring to the settlement. Most of the settlement was located just down from the spring, but the planning authorities insisted relocation to one of the highest points on the land, forty feet above the spring, out of sight from any public footpaths. Fortunately, the header tank and pipe run for a hydraulic ram pump were still intact and a new pump was installed. The hydraulic ram is a simple water pump, requiring no external energy, instead using the flow of the majority of the water to pump the remaining water uphill.

Much was done in the first few years and through necessity, or sometimes lack of experience, many structures were knocked together very quickly, as a short term solution. We are now in the next phase of development, where we are fortunate enough to have everything we need, but where much of the earlier

Extension to sawmill under construction

infrastructure is starting to decay and needs replacing. As time goes by we are gradually replacing the early building with longer term solutions and repairing the buildings which still have plenty of life in them. We now have the time to build things more substantially using the experience of what works and what does not.

The initial houses were all benders (simple structures made using bent hazel poles harvested from the coppice on the land) and were often clad using recycled marquee canvas from a nearby manufacturer. Other people lived in tents and the communal space was inside a yurt. Since then, the yurt has been replaced with a thatched roundhouse and most of the benders have been succeeded by slightly more substantial structures.

Most of the buildings are single storey and based round a frame made using round wood from Douglas fir tree tops; parts of the tree unsuitable for use in the sawmill. Simple notched joints are used to join the timbers, usually either as a roundhouse with reciprocal roof (a simple self supporting conical roof constructed using tree tops) or a simple rectangular frame with pitched roof. These are then clad with a variety of materials, often a combination: canvas, cob, straw bale or sawn timber (waney edged boards or stockading). The roofs are also clad with a variety of materials, including sawn timber, turf (with plastic liner), and corrugated iron.

We are concerned to improve the energy efficiency of our structures and are in the process of improving the insulation. There are varying levels of insulation, using sheep's wool, sawdust, old clothes and other recycled materials. Many of the houses were initially poorly insulated, due to time constraints at the time of construction, and, as we repair the structures, we are slowly upgrading the insulation to improve the efficiency.

More recently, a two storey timber framed guest house was built using sawn timber from our saw-mill and at the time of writing a small timber framed house is under construction.

The saw-mill itself is housed in a temporary barn, made using round wood and hay bale walls. Half of the roof is clad with recycled corrugated iron, the rest with canvas. This structure is slowly being replaced with a timber framed barn, using the timber from our site. The timbers have been cut in the sawmill and the frames are being constructed using only hand tools.

This has provided an opportunity to teach several volunteers the skills required for timber framing.

Income

Our cost of living is extremely low. We grow much of our own food and drinks. As we live fairly simple lives and buy few new possessions, it costs just over £100 per person per month to live here. We are all self employed and file tax returns where necessary, but no-one has ever earned enough to pay income tax.

We generate much of our income from selling our organic apple juice, made with apples grown in our orchards. The other main communal business is forestry.

The land contained two large orchards when the community began. The first of these orchards contains cooking apples, primarily Bramley's Seedlings. The other orchard consisted of a mix of dessert apples, primarily Cox's Orange Pippins and Egremont Russets. Many of the Cox trees were removed due to disease.

We recently received grants from Somerset County Council to plant new orchards. They are promoting the re-establishment of traditional orchards in Somerset. The first of these orchards comprises a variety of cider apple tree and the other orchard contains modern disease-resistant replacements for the Cox's. The new trees are traditional standard varieties; large trees whose first branches start above six feet. This makes them much more suitable for grazing animals and the orchards are easier to maintain with a scythe.

Initially, we sold the apples to shops and wholesalers, but they have a very short shelf-life. During bumper years, the market is usually flooded, as everyone else has a surplus too. After some time, we realised that apple juice not only has a longer shelf life, but also increases the value of the apples and provides an opportunity to promote ourselves in the local shops. Over the last few years, we have produced an average of 5,000 bottles per year, all with our own brand label.

The primary income of the forestry business is derived from sawn timber. Twenty acres of the woodland is conifer, mainly Douglas fir. The trees are felled using two-man hand saws and felling axes. The trunks are cleaned up and then cross-cut into 8ft to 16ft sawn logs, which are extracted from the woodland down to the sawmill using traditional cob horses and a logging arch.

The sawmill is powered by a 1937 wood-fired portable steam engine, which drives a belt-driven 1920s saw bench with a 4-ft circular saw. The off-cuts from milling the timber are seasoned and then provide most of the fuel required to power the engine. It is an old and temperamental setup, which makes it slow work, but we have no real alternative.

The timber is either sold or used on site. Most of the larch is used as fence posts for stock fencing and the Douglas fir is used for a wide range of projects around the land and in our homes. Currently much of the focus is on building the timber-framed barn to replace the current temporary sawmill barn.

There is also an opportunity to run small businesses, such as growing high value vegetables for sale, or furniture making.

More recently, we have started to earn a living through teaching. Traditionally, there has been some resistance here to using teaching as a source of income, as it is not directly involved in working the land. However, we have recently been teaching autistic children through practical work involving working on the land and in woodworking.

We also take volunteers, primarily through WWOOF (World Wide Opportunities on Organic Farms). Volunteers work 30 hours per week in exchange for food and accommodation. As well as a useful source of help for labour-intensive tasks (such as weeding, hay making and harvesting apples), we also find this a great way to teach people land-based skills and about sustainable living. Indirectly, involvement with WWOOFing is a means of communication with others involved in similar lifestyles and is a means of transferring useful traditional skills.

Goals
When the community was initially established, there was no common vision or goal. Although several members did have fairly similar visions, there were several conflicting dreams, which held back the progress of the community. At the very beginning there were those who wanted to establish agriculture on the land and those who wanted to conserve the land and buy food from the local shop. Some residents wanted no modern technology, whilst others wanted electricity and computers. At times, some residents have wanted the community to be open to anyone who wishes to

live here, whilst others have wanted the community to grow slowly and sustainably. For some residents the goals of the community were political, for others environmental and some just wanted to escape modern society.

Development of goals has been a long term process which has needed discussion over time. Today, everyone still has their own vision for the community and we still haven't defined a common goal, but these visions have converged and generally tend to be focused on environmental sustainability and working the land, both to earn a living and to provide much of our food needs. To some extent, we are so busy getting on with day to day living that there is no time for abstract views. Practicality of life leaves only limited time for such goals.

Earning a living from the land is a fundamental aspect of the community and this has shaped the direction that we have taken. It would have been very easy to get part-time jobs outside the community or to run courses, eco-retreats or a whole host of ventures on the land. Any of these would easily have covered our cost of living, but it has always been a goal to earn our living by working the land, traditionally. There are many people in this country who wish to work the land by hand and these days there are few places where this is possible, as most farms are now heavily mechanised. This is one of the primary reasons why people come here.

We have more land than is required for the subsistence of the community and it would be greedy and unfair not to share the products with others who do not have similar access. Additionally, there is a large area of land to maintain by hand, so we do need to spend a significant proportion of our time working it.

Whilst this goal has created many challenges, it forces us to work together as a community. The lack of income, but abundance of time also forces us to make do and mend rather than buy new.

Self-sufficiency has never been a formal goal of the community, but the food we buy in is our most significant negative contribution to climate change, even though we go to great pains to source the most ethical food we can get. Most of us are working hard to produce more of our own food and there has been much more focus on this aspect over the past few years. Recently,

Residential woodland dwelling

we started using horses to help cultivate the land, for the first time in several years, and hope that this will further reduce our imports.

Whilst we have a very low environmental impact, we are still dependant on the world around us, which is extremely unsustainable. This includes the highways we cycle over, the National Health Service which we occasionally rely on, and the internet. Until the rest of the world recognises the need to change and acts on it, we are unlikely to ever become completely sustainable, but our carbon footprint is a tiny fraction of the national average.

Conclusion

In its first twenty years, the community has had many ups and downs, with several conflicting characters. Often the people who get involved in projects such as this are strong-willed and they aren't always very communal types of people. Over recent years we have been careful to ensure social sustainability and have tried hard to attract people who will fit in with our approach. It feels like we are now in a good position and are gradually growing stronger every year.

Over the next few years, we intend to produce more food, including grains, beans and honey. We are planning to build a processing facility, so that we can sell more of our produce. We will continue replacing, repairing and enhancing our buildings. We will try to further improve our links with the local community. We hope to expand our businesses to the point where we don't need to find any work outside the community. And we hope that we can show others that it is possible to live happy and fulfilling lives, without destroying this beautiful planet.

Peter 'Pedro' Brace
has lived at Tinkers' Bubble for a number of years.

So What's New About Low-Impact Housing?

DENNIS HARDY

Did Plotlanders invent low-impact development on the flatlands of Essex and the shores of the South Coast nearly a century ago?

L ong before Essex became the slick place to live for 'City boys', it offered a popular refuge for generations of East Enders. From the end of the nineteenth century, for the best part of half a century (until the long arm of town planning put an end to all that), poor people found ways to build their own homes in the countryside.

Essex was ideal: it was close to London, it enjoyed fresh air blowing in from the North Sea, and land was cheap. When the farming industry went into depression, in the face of cheap imports from the New World, land prices plummeted – and nowhere more than in Essex. Farmers with no other source of income were only too happy to subdivide their fields and sell the plots to individual buyers. And for a down payment as little as £1, there was no shortage of buyers.

Saturday Afternoon
Until well into the last century, and in spite of legislation in 1912 enabling a full weekend at leisure, most people worked until Saturday lunchtime. The next day and a half was their own and a growing number of those who spent their weeks living in cramped basement flats and tenement blocks, under a seemingly permanent pall of smoke, could hardly wait to find their place in the sun. They travelled by bicycle or

train, loaded down with tools and building materials, eager to make a start.

Fred Gifford was one such émigré from the city, during the week a casual dock worker who, with an unreliable supply of work, was always short of money. What he lacked in income, though, he made up in determination, and somehow he scraped together enough to buy a plot of land for £10, in what is now London's Green Belt. The plot measured 100 by 40 feet and that was enough for him and his family to plan their dream home. It was 1934 when he became a landowner, and, like a lot of others, he took advantage of a surplus of bell tents left over from the First World War, to make a temporary home for his weekend endeavours. Each Saturday afternoon he could be seen cycling out from the East End with all manner of materials strapped to his back. There were rich pickings around the docks – bits of cast-off timber, packing cases, screws and nails – and plotlanders tell of how these found a new use. Everything had to be done for oneself and Fred soon sank a well in his garden to provide a fresh water supply. The end result of his labour was a narrow, timber-frame bungalow, built lengthwise on the site, with a front bay window. Appropriately, he pinned a sign on the gate to name it 'Perserverance' (sic). It was much later before the site was connected to mains services and his home remained throughout his lifetime without a made-up road and sewers.

'Perserverance' (sic) Bowers Gifford, Essex

For those who made a longer journey into the countryside, the train service from Fenchurch Street was the answer. Packed on weekdays with clerks coming in from the inner suburbs to the City, everything changed on a Saturday afternoon. Soon after lunch, one would see families boarding the trains that would take them beyond the metropolitan limits. Many of them would buy a ticket to Laindon, squeezing into the Third Class carriages with a clatter of buckets, carrying unwieldy planks of wood and trying to keeping an eye on their excited children. As the train drew in to the destination, the compartment doors would open and soon the platform was full as they jostled to leave the station and head across the fields to their treasured plots. Building a house requires many skills but there was always a neighbour on hand who knew how to cut a joist or fit a gutter. The new settlers were all individuals but a community of sort formed around their common endeavours.

And they all had a story to tell – like Mrs Granger, a doughty woman with a keen eye for this new opportunity to make a better life. Her first husband had a job as a caretaker in a block of London County Council flats. One day, in 1932, she spotted an advertisement in the evening paper for a plot of land costing £5, so she took her reluctant husband on the one shilling and twopence return train journey to Laindon, and they were persuaded by the agent to buy two adjoining plots to give themselves more space. She had to borrow a pound for the deposit and slowly paid it all back through instalments. Like Fred Gifford, a cheap army surplus tent was the first move, and each weekend they carried their own supply of fresh water, supplemented on site by rainwater strained through an old stocking for washing. Sometimes they rented the tent to boys from their estate in London, using the money to buy cement, sand and secondhand bricks.

Gradually their house rose from its footings and Mr Granger managed to get a transfer to an estate in Dagenham, within much easier reach of Laindon. In time, they reared chickens, geese and goats and bought a pony and trap. Eventually, gas was connected so they had all 'mod cons'. Their family grew and they were now able to buy a bigger house nearby, renting their original home to relatives during the Second World War when East London was the subject of enemy bombing. It had never been their expectation to make any money from their homes but, in due course, they moved to other houses in Essex, each time to a better one. As Mrs Granger later reflected, we never had a mortgage and it all started with a borrowed pound. 'I feel so sorry for young couples these days who don't get the kind of chance we had.'

The type of settlement described above became known as the plotlands. Sometimes they were tucked away in woodland, out of sight of officials, but more often they were clustered together in favoured locations like South Essex, where they were soon classified as a 'problem'. People were probably a lot healthier than their counterparts in London but the authorities feared epidemics from polluted water. An emergent planning lobby also decried the spoiling of the countryside in the face of these outbreaks of self-made homes. With the sale of land continuing, where, asked the protectionists, would it all end?

Knatts Valley, Kent

New Homes for Old

Making use of conventional building materials (whether bought legitimately or not) is always one way to build your own home. But the plotlanders were nothing if not inventive and it seemed that nothing was off limits. The conversion of redundant Victorian railway carriages, for instance, was a popular option, used quite widely but especially along the south coast. There it was the lure of a seaside location that enticed new users of old rolling stock. Sometimes a row of carriages appeared on the crest of sand-dunes, with an unrivalled view of the sea, and a few of these can still be seen today.

Railway carriages were well chosen. Not only were they cheap at the time, no longer needed for their original use, but they were also remarkably weatherproof. With a few adjustments inside they offered really snug homes, much loved by their owners. When it came to finding somewhere bigger it was not uncommon to buy a couple more carriages and pull them together into an 'H'-shape, all interlinked. Plots were bought for the same kind of price as those in Essex, and carriages were cheap and plenty. So, too, were old bus bodies and trams, an aircraft fuselage and even a cast-iron industrial boiler, which all lent themselves to some clever recycling. When the owners were not there, it was common to rent them to others, using the popular 'Dalton's Weekly' to advertise the property (like the following, which appeared in 1937):

HOLIDAYS – Winchelsea Beach. Double-deck, super Bus to let, excellently converted. Lge. verandah. Ckg, cabin. On private grd. Ample room for cars. Near Sea, shops. Accommodate 6-8. Ideal opportunity excel. holiday.

As well as an opportunity for people who were unable to buy their own home by any other means, this kind of quirky retreat appealed, too, to a different kind of user. Middle-class plotlanders were lured by the informality of these places, like the following correspondent who recalled with warmth her childhood holidays at Winchelsea Beach:

'A first holiday in a railway carriage converted into a bungalow; buying a plot of land nearby and the building of our own bungalow which was a rather superior model as I remember it – my father designed it like an 'E' without the middle stroke; my brother and I being kept out of mischief by the inspiration of filling the space under the floor-boards with tiny buckets of shingle (an endless task); of ruberoid on the roof, one section of which made the rainwater taste odd; the cess-pool and the chemical lavatory and the spiders in it; the smell of driftwood burning in the little kitchenette and of shrimps boiling; the catastrophe of having papered the tongue and groove bedroom walls when the paper split as the wood moved accord-

*ing to the termperature... the religious maniac
who used to call from a wooden shack to try and
save us; the cockneys who had the bungalow next
door (a railway carriage except for the porch); the
rather dashing people with fast cars who owned
'Four Winds' which was several railway carriages...
I remember the 'Old Ship' going into the sea when
the sea-wall burst and the bathing huts floating out
to sea and the tidal wave...'*

The sheer romanticism of it all also attracted artists
and others of a bohemian bent. There were no rules to
obey and a shack or converted carriage on the beach
was a dream come true. Before the First World War, the
sculptor Jacob Epstein, loved the peace of the coastal
hamlet of Pett Level, as did the painter Mark Gertler.
More recently, Derek Jarman lived with his partner
in a simple shack on a strip of shingle on Dungeness
Beach. Shoreham Beach in Sussex became a favourite
haunt of actors from London, who would often catch
the last train after their curtain call and hurry to one
of the converted carriages or huts that were scattered
across the island. Names like 'Cinderella' and 'Sleeping
Beauty', 'Rose Marie' and 'Lullaby' told their own story,
and the social life became legendary. Locals spoke
in awe of fast cars and weekend parties, extravagant
clothes and celebrities of the day.

Pett Level, East Sussex

In 1921 a contemporary observer of Shoreham Beach described an endless variety of styles. 'Some are fantastic, some grotesque, many are beautiful, and some are not.' Later, someone who spent his summer holidays there recalls what these places were like inside:

'Their wooden walls white-painted, with roofs of red or green, and verandahs open to the sea, the bungalows were not lacking in attraction or variety of design. Some were gabled, or had castellated tops, or towers to give them height, and other such elaborations. After dark, the soft glow of oil lamps filtered through chintzy curtains, while oil-heaters kept the evening chill at bay.'

For the plotlanders such places were paradise; for the authorities they were a perpetual problem – a health risk and a blot on the landscape. After the Second World War, local authorities were in a stronger position to rid the nation of this 'appalling mess' but the plotlanders were not without their champions in high places. Lord Mersey, chairing a House of Lords committee that looked at the future of Shoreham Beach, was more than sympathetic to the rights of individual homeowners. In what might now be regarded as a patronising view but was at the time interpreted as much-needed support, he requested that 'there must be adequate protection given to the small man who is being dispossessed... I am talking about the little man who has been content perhaps to live in a railway carriage. I should not care to live in a railway carriage myself, but there are people who are quite content with that.'

The end result across the country was that, even with new powers, it proved to be not so easy to remove what was already there. In the case of South Essex, it took New Town powers to do so, with the plotlands soon overlain by one of the postwar new towns (in this case, Basilldon). Elsewhere, although many of the plotlands remained, the concerns of the authorities were allayed as householders upgraded their properties and were, in time, connected to mains services. Meanwhile, with their new powers, the authorities were able to put a stop to fresh development of this kind. All of which brings us to a new generation of innovators, frustrated by conventional approaches to new housing and, like the plotlanders, determined to go it alone.

Plotlands in the Third Millennium?
Since the start of the present century (and even a few years before) a quiet revolution has been taking place. For all the talk about sustainable

housing, conventional developers have barely scratched the surface of what this really means. Better insulation, use of grey water and sourcing local materials are all well and good but it really amounts to little more than more efficient ways to accommodate the same old, unsustainable lifestyles. Certainly, it's a universe away from Simon Fairlie's much-used definition of 'development that, through its low negative environmental impact, either enhances or does not significantly diminish environmental quality', coupled with genuine attempts to achieve low-impact living. Around the country and more widely in Europe there is now a growing number of experiments designed to do just this.

Readers of *Diggers and Dreamers* will know of these experiments and of the difficulties the pioneer residents have had in trying to convince neighbours and local authorities of their serious intent. There are now, however, enough of these settlements and some are sufficiently well-established to enable a few general observations. In particular, how do they compare with the plotlands of yesteryear? Are these low-impact communities merely modern manifestations of an earlier experiment in self-built housing? The simple answer is that there are some points of similarity but also striking differences; history never makes it easy to match seemingly comparable events from different generations.

If we look first at the similarities, there are common issues of frustration, opposition, a commitment to self-build, and the use of marginal land. Firstly, both the plotlanders and today's low-impact proponents were fired by a sense of frustration with the mainstream housing market. For the plotlanders there was simply no other way to get a foothold on the housing ladder. Because agricultural land was cheap at the time and, with the help of a surplus of bell tents and redundant railway carriages, not to mention small loans repayable by regular instalments, even some of the poorest in society could turn their dreams into reality. Taking out a mortgage and buying a house on a new estate was simply not an option. For largely different reasons, the low-impact movement shares with the plotlanders a common source of frustration, in this case with the failure of governments and developers to pay more than lip-service to the idea of sustainability. Thus, like the plotlanders it was a case of self-help or nothing.

Secondly, the plotlanders and the low-impact enthusiasts alike soon came head-to-head with entrenched laws and hostile attitudes. In the former case, planning laws were still relatively weak and there was, in fact, little that could be done to stop new development. The situation is very different now and the use of land is very tightly controlled. That is why the proponents of low-impact housing have done well to recognise the fact, and, in certain instances, to negotiate local exceptions to general rules. In this way they can legitimately live on their own land in what is still widely regarded as unconventional development. There have been some famous victories in creating new opportunities with the blessing of the authorities, although it has to be said that these are still quite localised and always hard-fought.

A third similarity is that both the plotlanders and low-impact communities have been prepared to build their own homes. To be fair, in some cases the plotlanders took advantage of the likes of railway carriages and even ready-made sheds and larger units, but more often than not self-build was the order of the day. Moreover, in the case of the plotlanders because of cost and, for the low-impact builders a matter of principle, materials were often recycled and locally sourced.

Railway carriage being delivered to Shoreham Beach, Kent

Finally, the chances are that both plotlands and contemporary low-impact development will be found on marginal land. It was certainly marginal in farming terms (hence the low prices) and was often at risk of flooding and distant from services. This is not just a question of cost (although that is always a factor) but also because there is advantage in being off the beaten track, out of the public gaze. Some of the plotlanders were not bothered by this latter consideration but many consciously took the opportunity to find a place that offered privacy. Similarly, it is little surprise that low-impact communities will often be found in secluded valleys, in parts of the country where there are few other demands for the land.

In other respects, the two types of development could hardly be more different. For one thing, the plotlands were the product of a myriad of individual decisions. Neighbours will have chatted about their various experiences but it was by no means a collective movement. The trend started because generally poor people wanted a place of their own (often for weekends away in the first instance), and later they were joined by a bohemian set who thought it was all rather quirky. Low-impact settlers are far more likely to be driven by ideals than necessity, and will tend to ·be young with often middle-class backgrounds. They are innovators who are demonstrating in practice how society could come to terms with an urgent need to adopt sustainable ways of living. To that extent, and with the help of modern means of communication, it takes the form of a 'movement', in ways that the plotlanders could never contemplate. It is consciously part of 'alternative' society, whereas the plotlanders (in spite of their unconventional methods and the challenge they posed at the time) were, in political terms, inherently conservative, wanting little more than a place of their own.

A second difference is to be found in the changing circumstances of the two examples. The plotlanders had the advantage of being one step ahead of the authorities, who could do little more than throw up their hands in horror at the proletarian invasion of the countryside. Now, of course, with a panoply of regulations in place the odds are stacked against innovation. As a result, advocates of low-impact development have had to 'box clever', taking on the authorities on their own ground and finding ways to accommodate what they want within the law. They have been remarkably successful in doing so, although it is certainly an uphill struggle.

Jaywick Sands, Essex (Cover Photo Arcadia for All)

Yet another difference can be found in outcomes. The plotlanders were unashamedly people who wanted to better themselves. Like the story of Mrs Granger, she took every opportunity to trade upwards in the housing market. In other cases, homes that started out as very humble dwellings were added to and embellished when the means were available so that today they bear almost no resemblance to how they started. There are still railway carriages on Shoreham Beach, embedded in the frames of luxury bungalows with gable roofs and coloured tiles, coach lamps and security lights, and drives leading to double garages. This, quite clearly, is not the direction in which low-impact development will go. Their very ideology will ensure that not only will they remain much as they are but, with experience, they are likely to accommodate even more sustainable lifestyles.

It is certainly tempting to see these two forms of development as natural bedfellows. As shown above, there are indeed some similarities, but the differences, too, are very striking. The one was individually driven, the other a social movement. The rest, as they say, is history.

Dennis Hardy
is Emeritus Professor and Dean of the Australian institute of Business, he was previously Dean, Pro Vice-Chancellor and Deputy Vice-Chancellor of Middlesex University. He is author of a number of books on housing and planning including *Arcadia for All, Utopian England: Community Experiments 1900-1945* and *Alternative Communities in Nineteenth Century England.*

Arcadia for All: The Legacy of a Makeshift Landscape by Colin Ward and Dennis Hardy. A study of the history of the plotlands from Canvey Island to Jaywick Sands, and from Peacehaven to Pitsea. Available from Five Leaves (www.fiveleaves.co.uk)

Eco-mobile

CHRIS COATES

*Mobile home parks can bypass much housing legislation,
but does eco-snobbery stop aspiring low-impact dwellers from
considering this option?*

I say, I say, I say! What's the difference between a mobile home park and a low-impact development?

Answer: one is a form of development clearly understood by the planning authorities and regularly granted planning permission across the country on sites that would otherwise be refused permission for housing – and the other isn't.

Of course there are a few other differences and a huge cultural chasm between the two, but on examination the differences start to look rather smaller than at first glance. When I was 12, I had a school friend whose family lived for a while in a set of what I can only describe as permanent tents (a series of frame tents with wooden floors joined by canvas corridors) in a large clearing in Swithland Woods in Leicestershire. There were other chalets and caravans arranged around the edge of the field, but I can't remember now whether they were occupied permanently. My friend's family eventually moved into a "proper" house when his father found work as the local gravedigger, a job that came with a house in the cemetery. I forgot about the little settlement in the forest, until a few years ago when I happened to be out walking in the Charnwood area and stumbled across a thriving little community of now somewhat more substantial chalets looking well cared for and certainly well used. The big differ-

ence was in the occupants. No longer was it a shelter for unemployed families and there was nothing that could be called a "permanent tent". By the look of the cars parked outside them, these were occupied by middle income or retired couples enjoying a weekend rural retreat or their retirement in the countryside. Somewhere along the way from the late 1960's, what had once been a housing option of last resort became a desirable retirement home in the countryside, almost certainly fetching a price well beyond anything a low income family could afford today.

Having spent years looking unsuccessfully for a plot for a group self-build scheme I was intrigued by these chalets in the woods. Despite the housing crash, building plots still go for silly money, making affordable self-build pretty much a pipedream, and I wondered whether there was any way you could build anything similar to these chalets today. I started to do some research into what I now know are called "Park Homes" or mobile home parks. I wanted to know quite what constituted a mobile home: are we just talking glorified caravans here? Courtesy of a government website I got a very interesting answer. A mobile home turns out to be a single-storey structure, up to 111 square metres floor area (see box), designed for people to live in which is physically capable of being moved along the highway either by being towed or else in no more than two sections on the back of large trucks. I later found out that the ability to move was largely theoretical as, in practice, once they are on site they are very rarely moved again.

A quick conversation with the local planning office confirmed what I thought: that mobile home parks are not seen as housing developments and so can utilise land not designated for housing in local plans.[1] They are granted 25 year renewable planning consents and turn out to be regulated by a licence issued by the local Environmental Health Department. A couple of emails got me a copy of our local licence (they are probably broadly the same everywhere, but check out your local council for details). The licence mainly seemed to be concerned with imposing some basic fire protection conditions; minimum distances between homes and provision of communal fire extinguishers. This worry about fire would appear to be due to mobile homes not having to comply with the building regulations. There is a fairly new British Standard for Residential Park Homes – BS 3632:1995 which sets some basic standards for construction. The rest of the licence and other regulations, The Mobile Homes Act 1983 and more recent legislation all relate to how the site is managed.

What is the legal definition of a 'mobile home'?

The law defines both 'mobile home' and 'caravan' as: "any structure designed or adapted for human habitation which is capable of being moved by road from one place to another (whether by being towed, or by being transported on a motor vehicle or trailer) and any motor vehicle so designed or adapted'. The connection of mains water / electricity / sewerage or addition of cosmetic skirts that do not fix the structure to the ground do not prevent it from coming within the definition."

The definition excludes: railway stock on rails forming part of the railway system, and tents.

However, it includes:

- *conventional caravans and mobile homes*
- *dormobiles*
- *touring caravanettes, and*
- *adapted railway carriages.*

A large, twin-unit caravan may come within the definition if it: is composed of not more than two separately made sections, and is capable of being transported by road when assembled, and does not exceed 60 feet (18.288 metres) in length, 20 feet (6.096 metres) in width, and 10 feet (3.048 metres) from the floor to the ceiling internally.

Chalets with roofs and porches may come within the definition.
Taken from Shelter website: http://england.shelter.org.uk/get_advice/eviction/eviction_from_mobile_homes/mobile_homes_-_definitions

DIY 'mobile home' Findhorn 2013

> *"One of the advantages of a mobile home park is that it can bypass much of the housing legislation. Once you have permission for a site you can bring on anything that meets the definition of mobile home, which allows for a multitude of sins and virtues. If it is a commercial site you have to conform to the design standards laid down in BS3632, but you don't have to comply with building regs or apply for permission for each unit."*
> Simon Fairlie[2]

Reading through all this bureaucratic bumf I was struck by the strange similarities between these rules and regulations and those of emerging cohousing groups. Each unit is in individual leasehold ownership with the right to sell/inherit etc.

The sites are in single ownership, usually private, and there has been concern about abuse by unscrupulous landlords exploiting mobile home owners. Surely there is no reason sites couldn't be owned by a co-operative, or company where the members own the site collectively. Or even by a Community Land Trust. There is an assumption that there will be communal facilities provided and often the social community side is the big selling point in commercial park home sites publicity. This is co-housing in all but name. Except instead of each unit costing £120,000+ to build they could surely be in the £40-£60,000 range. Or even less if you did self-build.

The Segal Self-Build Trust spent many of its early years vigorously denying that a timber-frame Segal style house was "nothing more than a mobile home in disguise", in order to persuade Housing Associations to work with it. But with a modest change in design so that it could be brought onto site in two sections I can't see any reason why a Segal building or similar would not fit the legal definition of a mobile home. You could then have a well-insulated, high environmental spec, decent sized Eco-Park Home that is affordable and could get planning permission on land not designated for housing. Sounds too good to be true?

In the back of my mind I had a memory that I had seen a version of what I was trying to visualise, on holiday somewhere in a quiet backwater of a seaside resort, or tucked away down a farm track by the side of a secluded lake. Then on a visit to interview members of the spiritual community at Findhorn I realised I was standing in the middle of an old style residential caravan park that was slowly transforming itself into an Eco-trailer park all disguised as a spiritually based eco-village. Here was what I was looking for. Clearly there are other eco-houses and buildings at Findhorn but fundamentally, in planning terms, it is a residential caravan park with various add-ons and extensions. Within the residential caravan park part of the site a program is underway which will replace the ageing energy inefficient caravans and 1960's chalets, with a

Modern 'mobile home' Findhorn 2013

Developer built 'mobile home' Findhorn 2013

variety of eco-mobile homes. They are doing it without having to apply for planning permission because, in planning terms, they are replacing 'like-with-like', a mobile home with another mobile home. Neither do the new eco-homes require building control certification. The replacement homes range from slightly quirky self-designed and self-built units right through to contractor built units – definitely at the eco-posh end of the mobile home spectrum.

Some British manufacturers are gradually cottoning on to the benefits of good quality, well insulated mobile homes. Quercus Rural Building Design have worked on a range of projects that fall under this criteria[3]. And some of the homes going up at Findhorn are being constructed by local firm Green Leaf Design & Build.

Perhaps the biggest obstacle to Eco-Park Homes popping up across the country would appear to be eco-snobbery. Lots of people I've mentioned the idea to really can't cope with the idea of being eco-trailer trash, or even eco-trailer posh! The thought of living on what amounts to a souped-up caravan site simply doesn't have the eco-cred of a BedZED or a Strawbale cottage in a low impact eco-village development. In reply I would suggest that rather than seeing Eco-Park Homes as an

extension of caravan culture we perhaps look on them as licensed plotlands (see article about the Plotlands Movement, p67) – a chance to reinvent that classic urban escape route, not this time from the slums of early 20th century cities but instead from the crazy overheated housing market of the early 21st century.

DIY 'mobile home' Findhorn 2013

A version of this article appeared in the Spring/Winter 2006 issue of *The Land* magazine.

Chris Coates
is President/Chair of the International Communal Studies Association and author of *Communes Britannica: a history of communal living in Britain 1939-2000*. He is a founder member of Forgebank Cohousing project.

Creative 'mobile home' Findhorn 2013

Notes

1 Note, however, that some local development plans have a policy stating that permission for mobile home sites will be given on the same basis as permission for housing.

2 Article by Simon Fairlie, first published in *Building for a Future*, Autumn 2005

3 British manufacturers are gradually cottoning on to the benefits. Peter Caunt, of Quercus has already installed an example of his larch-clad Heartland timber chalet, made in Scotland from both Scottish and Scandinavian timber, at Dalraddy Holiday Park, near Aviemore in Scotland.

Contacts:

National Park Home Council:
www.nationalcaravan.co.uk
Telephone 01252 318251

National Association of Park Home Residents
www.naphr.co.uk
Telephone 01492 535677

Independent Park Home Advisory Service (IPHAS) www.iphas.co.uk

Park Home Legal Services
Telephone 01275 373762

Quercus Rural Building Design
http://www.quercusrbd.co.uk

Green Leaf Design & Build
http://www.greenleafdb.co.uk

Key development stages: Lammas

PAUL WIMBUSH

From vision to reality, Paul outlines the steps taken to realise the Lammas ecovillage.

The concept of the Lammas ecovillage was born around a campfire at a summer festival. Was there something different about this chance gathering that propelled the project forwards to proceed? If so it was simply commitment. In particular the resolve on the part of a small group of visionaries to pursue the concept with drive and vigour, come what may. We had no financial backing, no experience of housing development, and were all engaged in other projects that required large time and energy commitments.

What we did have was experience of community living – and this inspired us to put together a model that we felt would stand the test of time. We were keen to create something that enabled social independence whist fostering a strong sense of community. It would need to be affordable and financially secure to give us any chance of attracting residents. We also wanted a template that could be scaled up and replicated if proven successful.

In retrospect Lammas' evolutionary journey passed through five distinct phases. I have found it very useful to define and share these stages because they provide a roadmap that other individuals and groups might benefit from.

1: The Vision

Our first task was to define what it was that we wanted to create. In order to do this we formed a 'core group' to steer the project, making decisions by agreement. There were five of us to begin with and we made a good team, drawing on each others' strengths and naturally occupying different and complementary roles within the project.

Our intention was clear – we wanted to get prior planning permission for a model ecovillage development, setting a precedent which others could follow. We aimed to create a development that, whilst being rooted in the land, integrated itself with the wider community. We wanted to create a bridge of opportunity for people in mainstream lifestyles to create a sustainable land-based lifestyle for themselves.

Our vision was that the land would undergo a radical transformation. Human-scale farming would shape the landscape, creating a diverse patchwork of forest-gardens, crops, orchards, and ponds with plenty of woodland for fuel, shelter and wildlife. The houses, barns and greenhouses, all self-built using natural building techniques, would merge into the landscape. We planned to create a network of permissive footpaths throughout the development to ensure the residents, along with local people and casual visitors, would be able to access the landscape and experience the reality of this new landscape first hand.

In order to succeed we were aware that we would need to recruit residents for the project along with a wide support base to assist us with setting the project up. As a core group we articulated our intentions with an outline proposal; basically an A4 document that described our vision. In fact this document went through various incarnations as our clarity emerged. This was published on our newly formed website. We gathered a mailing list of interested parties and kept them up to date with our progress through regular newsletters (which continue to this day). We also gave presentations about the project, wrote articles for local newspapers and began working with Undercurrents Video on an internet mini-series.

All in all we had set ourselves a clear brief, and were making practical steps to move forwards. Whereas Lammas was initially driven by a voluntary core group, some of whom intended to live in the ecovillage and others who contributed from a place of altruism, there are many other approaches that forming groups might take. These range from a developer-led scheme with a defined product (eco-smallholding plot within an ecovillage) to a resident-led scheme in which people contribute financially and practically in an agreed equitable manner.

2: The Structure
As time went on, the concepts behind our ecovillage project were developed in more detail and an unincorporated association was formed to take the project forward. Associations are really useful legal structures for new groups – they are easy to create, easy to run and enable a project to have its own identity. The right people appeared at the right times and step by step the dream of Lammas was shaped. The project seemed to grow a life and a will of its own, manifesting the necessary stepping stones for progress to be made.

The initial concept drawing resembled a cartwheel in which 25 dwellings were clustered around a central village green and people's gardens and fields radiated outwards. The houses were accessed by a circular track that ran behind the dwellings and intersected the fields. Thus the village green was the conceptual meeting point for all, accessible only on foot. This model was based on the success of the layout at Holtsfield (near Swansea) in generating a strong sense of community. We were aware that this conceptual layout would need to morph considerably when applied to a real landscape.

We spent a long time looking at examples of how much land people needed to support themselves. To a degree the size of the household and the quality of the land are variable factors in this. It is however the choice of livelihood that is pivotal to determining the size of a holding. Many land-based enterprises (bees, butterflies and buttons for example) do not need much space, whilst others (cows, charcoal and cabbages for example) require lots of land. I currently advise that 3 acres is a minimum size for a single person and 5 acres for a couple/ family – this allows for an acre of biomass (to keep warm/ cook with), an acre for your house/ veg-garden/ orchard, and some land dedicated to livelihood.

Building the Hub roof using recycled materials and voluntary help

We were very aware that we were pioneering something new and we were very keen to create enough momentum from within the project to enable a supportive social network to develop. In exploring how many households we needed to create an optimum community population, we again looked at other working models for inspiration. We considered that eight dwellings was an absolute minimum in order to maintain an alternative culture. We noticed that a community can consist of up to (about) 25 dwellings, and when numbers increase above that level then notional sub-communities tended to form; Tipi Valley (with three distinct sub-communities), and Sandy Lane (with multiple clusters of chalets) provided good examples of this trend. We decided that ideally we wanted approximately twenty smallholdings to gain enough momentum and diversity to launch and maintain the project.

The settlement's legal structure was based upon the conventional village model, allowing people social freedom to participate in community if and when they chose. People would buy into the project and then could sell up if they wanted to leave. Households would thus be able to benefit from their investments in terms of land health, biodiversity, built structures and infrastructure. We were very clear that we did not want to create an intentional community in the traditional sense of the term. One of our guiding principles was that people should be able to come and live at Lammas and never be under any obligation to attend a single community meeting, work-day or gathering (the hermit principle). The framework would be as liberal as possible, provided that residents met the broad principles of low-impact development. This framework, laid out as a result of the planning process, would clearly define the legal requirements for both the residents and the organisation.

There were some elements that we considered best held in common: trackways, a village green, woodland, common grazing. In order to make provision for the care and maintenance of these in an equitable way Lammas would levy a service charge to cover such costs. It would then offer any employment firstly to residents, thus enabling people to make their contribution to the community in money or labour, depending on what work needed doing.

Lammas soon became 'Lammas Low-impact Living Initiatives Ltd', a 'Co-operative registered under the Industrial and Provident Society Act 1965 for the benefit of the Community'. This archaic legal structure is part co-operative, part charity and part business. We chose this route because we were clear that we wanted the project to have a remit that was much wider than the ecovillage at its core. This was a response to the tendency observed amongst many alternative communities to become unduly introspective.

Whereas previously the project had been managed by a self-elected core-group, with the change in legal status we moved to a larger decision making body and elected a committee of directors. Decisions were largely made by consensus, though we reserved the option to revert to a majority vote on those occasions when we could not reach agreement.

Lammas had thus moved from a concept to a scheme with a defined set of parameters that included a two-tier legal structure (that gave autonomy and security to residents whilst enabling a guardian entity to oversee the project and manage the common areas and services), clarity on the number and nature of the households along with the relative size of the plots, and an agreed approach to planning (attaining prior approval through a newly launched low-impact development policy).

3: Land

There are many ways to locate land suitable for a project. The conventional route is through estate agents. Most areas tend to have estate agents that specialise in farming properties and land. Another approach is simply through local connections – the land sales taking place 'off the books' without any advertising. It is definitely worth approaching farmers and local people in an area if you are clear that you want to be in a particular region.

With Lammas we were clear that we needed to be in Pembrokeshire – because at the time that was where the first low-impact development policy was launched. It is slightly different now in that the low-impact policy covers the whole of Wales. In theory you can apply for a 'One-Planet Development' (OPD) as it is now called, anywhere in the country, though it is worth being aware that areas of special designation (National Parks for example) often have local policies that also need complying with.

Land is averaging about £6000 an acre at the moment. For an OPD application, you will need land that has some prospect of being self-sufficient in water, and would benefit from land that has a reasonable aspect (east, south or west) and is not unduly overlooked.

In Lammas we found land through advertising. This is a somewhat unorthodox route but we are not alone in having succeeded with it. We toured Pembrokeshire with a series of talks to launch the project, and advertised these in the local papers. Following this, we had a phone call from a lady, Su, who explained that she had the perfect site for us: 200 acres of south facing pasture in North Pembrokeshire, with a spring, woodland and a hydro turbine.

After several visits we decided to commit to the land. This was not without reservation from within the group – the site was very exposed to wind and had become very degraded after 25 years of grazing. Nonetheless we proceeded to root our dreams at Pont y Gafel farm. Su agreed to hold the land ready for us to purchase at a later date.

Having found a site we were then able to move forwards into the design stage. Securing a site was an important step forwards in enabling prospective residents to assess whether our project was what they were looking for. In order to be clear about relative levels of commitment from prospective residents we asked people to write draft plot plans and put down financial down-payments sufficient to cover the cost of the planning appli-cation. This turned out to be a valuable process in helping people decide whether to stay with the project or not.

At this point we initiated a dialogue with the local community. With Su's help we invited all the Pont y Gafel neighbours to tea and cake at the farmhouse so that we could share our ideas for the project. About a dozen people came and there was a very mixed reaction to our plans. A few of the local residents were very supportive. Many were not. In the spirit of openness and fostering good neighbourly relations we followed this initial meeting with an open day at Pont-y-gafel farm, inviting all local people in the area to gather so that we might explain and discuss the project. We had invited a supportive researcher to facilitate the event, and we cleared out a large agricultural shed to host the gathering. As the day unfolded it became apparent that many local people felt very threatened by the idea of an ecovillage on their doorstep. So much so that following our open day an anti-Lammas campaign group formed.

Ultimately the adversity generated from local community relations led to a strengthening and a tightening of our plans. One of the biggest concerns of the local people was the scale of the project. In an attempt to hear and respond we split the development into two phases. We would apply for the first phase of nine households at this stage and would not develop plans for a second phase until the nine households had established themselves and satisfied the planners that they were providing positive environmental, social and economic benefit. We did what we could to address other concerns, though we seemed unable to influence the entrenched local opposition.

Having reached a point where our proposals were becoming sufficiently defined to give us confidence and clarity, we then entered the planning system.

4: Planning

The OPD policy in Wales requires a large amount of very detailed planning. Whilst this could be viewed as evidence of a draconian bureaucratic system pre-occupied with control, it would be more productive to view it as an invaluable opportunity to properly prepare yourselves for what will probably be an enormous and ambitious transition from mainstream living to land-based self reliance. The time and energy invested at this stage of the process will prepare the ground for effectively manifesting the project later on.

For those unfamiliar with the OPD planning policy, there are several key requirements that are expected of applicants:

- Households must harvest their water needs from the site.

- Households must be self-reliant in (renewable) heating fuel and electricity generation.

- Households will be expected to demonstrate an ecological footprint as low as 2.4 global hectares per person (see **www.wikipedia.org/wiki/ecological_footprint** for more information) and work towards a one-planet footprint.

- All construction must be zero carbon in construction and use.

- Households must meet their basic household needs from land-based livelihoods within five years. In addition to a self-reliant lifestyle, this translates to approximately £3000 income per adult per annum from land based activities. Over and above that residents are free to supplement incomes by other means (so long as that doesn't include excessive travel).

In Lammas we employed a permaculture consultant to help us move from a place of spatial concepts to a well considered design for the site. She facilitated a series of design workshops in which we studied the many different aspects of the project: soil, weather, view, flow patterns for people, water flows, wildlife, services, social patterns, etc.

One of the aspects that we spent a long time looking at was our interface with the wider world. We were aiming to strike a careful balance between the privacy of residents and the needs of visitors to explore and understand what the project was about. In looking at other models, an attractive precedent was provided by Holtsfield in which a village green, large picnic table, and notice board served as a community centre. The big benefit with this arrangement was that the ongoing inputs required were very minimal. On the other hand the hostel at Brithdir Mawr had provided a very user-friendly interface along with an income stream for the project. We knew that being the first ecovillage of its kind we would have lots of people wanting to visit. We reasoned that it would be best to make provision for these visitors and to create a mutually beneficial arrangement whereby we could generate some income, both for the residents and the organisation, in return for an educational and rewarding experience. We reckoned that a venue to accommodate this would become invaluable and, employing the services of an architect, designed a turf-roofed, timber-framed, natural building which would be flexible enough to adapt to multiple uses.

We were then faced with the task of allocating plots to residents. We had aimed to establish an allocation process that would engage people in such a way that if they did not get a plot, they would nonetheless be empowered by the process. What surprised us all was that events seemed to work out perfectly, in that we were able to allocate nine plots to committed and passionate people without turning anybody away. The process was designed so that by the point at which plots were allocated, everybody had made significant headway in developing their ideas and plans and presenting them in a format ready for the planning application. We had created a self-selecting process based entirely on the viability of plans and levels of commitment. This point is important to understand because it expresses the core distinction between intentional community and the traditional village model. At no point were value judgements made about people's personalities or lifestyle choices. As long as people were willing to work within the planning frameworks and were sufficiently committed to meet the paperwork requirements (which needed to stand up to significant scrutiny) they were welcome. The process of compiling the plot management plans had, in itself, sorted the sheep from the goats.

Volunteers help with the construction of a house

We continued to develop and articulate the vision, both through our website and by touring festivals with a display stand. We also held occasional gatherings which were a good opportunity to communicate and get to know each other as a group. Whilst we did not have any clear expectations I think we were surprised at who the project attracted. People came from all over the UK, with an incredibly diverse set of backgrounds. Katy and Leander were living in a terraced house in Liverpool, with Leander working as a botanist for Manchester museum and Katy as a children's book illustrator. Ayres and Marianne were living in a first floor flat in Bath. Ayres, having previously been a US marine, now worked as a body therapist. Some people had bountiful experience of low-impact living. Many had none. People's reasons for joining the project were as diverse as their backgrounds. Some were motivated by the prospect of a better life for their children, others for the chance of an affordable natural home. One thing I learnt from this process was that you cannot pre-judge people, for they are often full of surprises.

Meanwhile we were tying down how the finances would work in the project. This was challenging in that none of us had any experience of large-scale developments. Nonetheless, keen to install a comprehensive infrastructure network that would stand the test of time, we costed out the trackways, water and electricity networks as best we could. We anticipated being able to secure some funding for the community hub and hydro scheme and endeavoured to keep the plot prices as low as we could, setting the cost of a plot at £35,000. To put this into context there was a building plot for sale in the local village at the time; it was approximately one tenth of an acre and had outline planning permission. It was on the market for £130,000.

We assembled a good planning application, which was refused by local planners. We then strengthened those aspects of the application that were considered lacking and resubmitted our plans to a backdrop of local opposition. This was in turn refused and we simply kept bouncing back. We spent just over three years in the planning system. We were led a merry dance by the local planners and paid the price for our naivety. When we managed to appeal, things proceeded at a much better pace.

OPD projects are normally refused planning at a local level. Fortunately in Wales there is a fairly good

Low impact hay-bale house

Planning Inspectorate which handles appeals to the Welsh Government. As a guide I would suggest that a planning application should take about six months to write, should cost about £2000 to £3000 and you should get a decision within six to twelve months (assuming that you will be refused at a local level and will appeal).

Each step of the process builds on those that have come before. If you are committed and thorough I do not see any reason why you should fail at the planning stage. If you do, however, the system is designed to be sufficiently flexible for you to re-apply, addressing any points that were considered lacking in the previous round.

5: Manifestation

Following on from planning permission you will enter the most challenging phase. You will have five years to set up and demonstrate a land-based sustainable lifestyle. To achieve this you will need to create a supportive infrastructure quickly and effectively. Be as gentle as you can upon yourselves, for this is a huge task that requires dedication. Sustaining human energy is an important part of the picture. People living in sub-standard accommodation are much more prone to stress that those who have created a comfortable transition. One of the biggest tasks will be building the dwellinghouse. By this point you will already have a design – but do not hesitate to evolve it if need be. At the end of the day you will need to live with your design choices. It is a fabulous opportunity to express yourself, though bear in mind bigger is not always better. It is always surprising just how much time, money and energy is poured into every inch of floor space. It is also worth recognising that simplicity equates to expediency when it comes to building, just as attention to detail equates to longevity.

The project will become a big building site for the first few years and it really pays to organise things carefully. There is nothing more frustrating than having to move a pile of topsoil/ timber/ sand more than once because it is in the way. It is difficult to hold-back from planting trees – just bear in mind you will need to work around them once they are in. Incidentally, young trees are slow to establish in grassland and will establish themselves much quicker if mulched well.

A low-impact lifestyle is undoubtedly more physical than the sedentary lifestyles common to the modern world, but be careful not to over-exert your body. Choose ways of doing things which require minimum effort. It is easier to create a vegetable plot by mulching well in advance of planting potatoes rather than simply digging out the turf, though this approach requires patience and planning. Volunteer input can magnify your labour capability tenfold, but will need very careful management. Volunteers are at their best when they are comfortable, well fed and working on a task they find fulfilling. Using plant machines requires equal diligence. Diggers are remarkable tools that can move mountains of earth and make a horrendous mess at the same time. They do have a place in building a sustainable infrastructure – particularly within the timescales that we are working in.

You will have many choices to make as a group and issues will undoubtedly arise that will be challenging. Trust the structures that you have put into place. At the end of the day intention is everything.

In myself and in many others I have observed that there comes a point when your infrastructure begins to support you. One day you will be eating your own-grown food in your own off-grid dwelling warmed by your own fuel. You will recognise that you will have created something of real value for future generations. You will know at this point that the long journey was well worth it.

Paul Wimbush
is the founder of the Lammas ecovillage. He has a wealth of experience in alternative community models. He has been active in influencing planning policy both at a local and national level. He supports community groups and individuals in setting up low-impact developments and in negotiating projects through the planning system.

Paul's book *The Birth of an Ecovillage – Adventures in an Alternative World* explores the many contributing elements and opposing forces behind the creation of a pioneering settlement that empowers people to recreate their relationship with the natural world. It is available as a book or e-book from the Lammas website: **www.lammas.org.uk**

Life afloat

TONY SMETHAM

Tony, a London-based boater, introduces us to a group of people taking to the waterways to reduce their housing costs

There are around 2,200 miles of canals in Britain. They were originally built in the 18th and 19th centuries, forming the equivalent of the motorway network during the industrial revolution. Nowadays, these canals, along with about 1,000 miles of navigable rivers, have become home to perhaps as many as 15,000 people, living in what has been described as "the longest village". Each new mooring place promises meetings with old friends not seen for months or making the acquaintance of new ones, and there is a camaraderie on the waterways now all but lost amongst land dwellers.

Although a life afloat isn't necessarily inherently "low-impact", boat dwellers are forced to be aware of where everything they use comes from, how long it lasts and where it goes. Water, gas, electricity, heating and waste all have to be provided for, even in the depths of winter, when canals can be frozen for weeks on end. And with storage at a premium on all but the biggest of boats, boaters have to be ruthless about getting rid of every unnecessary piece of household junk.

Individual boats can range from power-hungry beasts with all the gadgets normally found in land-based homes to lean, green energy saving machines. Many boats moored in marinas have access to mains electricity and water, which means they can have washing

Solar panels, bike storage and plants make good use of this boat's roof

machines, fridges and the like on board. Away from marinas, though, all boaters have to be frugal with their resources as all electricity has to be generated on board and other resources such as water and rubbish bins could be a day's journey away.

Most boats are equipped with a bank of lead acid batteries for supplying electricity to power onboard equipment. These are generally charged by alternators driven by the engine, but solar panels are a common addition to many boats. Some boaters also use wind generators but these tend to be a much less reliable power source than solar panels, so they are not popular.

Most boats are able to generate mains electricity, either via an inverter connected to the batteries or using a separate generator. But it is more efficient to use electricity directly from the batteries, so many boaters use 12V versions of electrical appliances wherever possible. Also, the boater's nose for a power supply is legendary – whenever a group of boaters meet up in a pub or cafe, there is invariably a tangle of cables leading to an array of phones, laptops, battery chargers etc.

The engine is one aspect of living aboard that can hardly be described as low-impact. Virtually all boats have diesel engines, and there is little that can be done to reduce the environmental impact of these. One manufacturer boasts that its engines can run on used engine oil, although they don't suggest that it is a good idea.

One boater made a quite determined attempt to modify her engine to run on waste vegetable oil. She found a company that was prepared to design a system to deal with all the problems that were specific to boat engines but they were ultimately defeated by not being able to get the oil hot enough to work safely. So it seems that there may be no alternative to fossil fuels for the time being.

Most modern boats, perhaps not surprisingly, have water-cooled engines, usually using the canal as a plentiful supply of coolant. Typically, the water that cools the engine also passes through the hot water tank to ensure a supply of hot water after running the engine for only a relatively short time. Some boaters have also devised fan heaters, using recycled car parts to put even more of the waste heat from the engine to good use.

Lighting is one area in which boaters have been pioneering low-power solutions. The need to preserve battery life has meant that boaters are always searching for the most efficient form of lighting. The fluorescent lights that would have been found on many boats only a few years ago are being replaced by LED lighting. They have become so popular that at least two boat-based businesses have been started specialising in LED lighting.

One feature that sets boaters apart from their land-based cousins is their willingness to discuss toilet facilities. Until recently, boaters were divided into those who favoured chemical toilets and the ones with toilets using a holding tank that needs to be pumped out. To this choice has been added the possibility of using composting toilets. A variety of commercial models are available, but many boaters make their own composting loos using buckets and sawdust.

One exciting development in the field of composting toilets is LooWatt. This is a waterless toilet developed originally for use in the third world where drinking water is at a premium. It is used in conjunction with an anaerobic digester to convert human waste into biogas, which is mainly methane, and fertiliser. The methane can either be used to run a boiler or to power a generator to produce electricity. One of the team developing this system is a boater, and the toilet has been designed to work within the confines of a narrowboat. Once the system goes into commercial production, there will doubtless be many customers from within the boating community.

Boaters tend to be pretty resourceful folks, and have devised simple solutions to many of the issues they face. For example, the roof of a narrowboat is an ideal space for collecting rainwater, which can be used for watering plants or, with suitable filters, for cooking, washing and drinking. Also, the baseplate is in constant contact with cold water. This provides boats with a cool area that serves as a perfectly good alternative to a refrigerator in all but the hottest weather. Running a fridge places a heavy load on the boat's batteries, so this is a valuable saving for many people.

Continuous Cruisers
Generally speaking, there are two types of boaters living on Britain's canals and rivers. Many live on residential moorings in marinas, often with water and electricity provided. These moorings need residential planning permission, so they are in short supply and demand for them is high, particularly in densely populated areas. Rather than live in marinas, many people choose to live without a mooring, travelling around the waterways as "continuous cruisers".

The law governing the use of the canals allows anybody to moor anywhere on the towpath side of the canal network for up to two weeks at a time. There is nothing to say how far a boat must move after that, only a stipulation that it must be used "bona fide for navigation". This is one of the most hotly debated topics on the canals. On one side, there are those who believe it was a terrible oversight to fail to define a minimum distance people must move. Opposing them are those who think it was a deliberate omission, intended to allow people to live on the canals as they see fit, so long as they keep moving every so often.

One place where this has an impact is London where there are about 60 miles of canals and rivers within reach of the Underground network. This means that liveaboard boaters are able to comply with the navigation requirement while still remaining within the London area. So, for many people a little planning can mean that a nomadic life afloat can be combined with a full-time job in London.

One result of this has been a dramatic increase in the popularity of boating as a housing option in the capital. As the cost of housing, whether to buy or to rent, has spiralled, more people have taken to the canals as a way of saving money. Many people have welcomed this growth in the floating population. The government have even offered incentives to local councils to increase the number of moorings available. But there has also been opposition, particularly from the navigation authority, who regard the expanding floating population as causing congestion.

In 2011, British Waterways released proposals that would have forced boaters in the London area to move more often and over a wider area. These were unpopular, not just with boaters but with anglers, canoeists, rowers and all the other people who would have been inconvenienced by the extra boat movements. The result was that boaters came together to form two groups in two neighbouring areas to oppose the proposals. Several hundred people attended meet-

A number of boats to spell the word "HOME", to make the point that the canals are our home (photo: Katrin Thomas)

Probably the smallest liveaboard boat in the country

ings to protest against the proposals, and organised detailed research to demonstrate that the proposals were unnecessary, unworkable and did not achieve their intended purpose.

The immediate result of this work was that the proposals were overturned. But it also achieved tremendous results in bringing boaters together to form a more organised community. Several of us saw the potential of this organised group and attempted to harness it to develop some of the facilities we need that land-based people take for granted.

Community
The growth of the liveaboard community in London means it encompasses an ever-widening cross-section

of society. This has led to many of the same problems as are found in land-based communities. Although for some a life afloat may be a lifestyle choice offering an escape from the cost of renting, for others it is the last rung on the housing ladder above homelessness. Poverty, illness and unemployment can conspire to prevent people from being able to carry out repairs and maintenance to their boats when needed. This can result in boats sinking or breaking down and being unable to move.

Although the Canal and River Trust will usually have a degree of patience with people who find themselves unable to comply with the navigation requirements, some people may still ultimately face losing their homes if they do not move far enough. The Waterways Chaplaincy service, run by the Salvation Army, have been of immense help to boaters, particularly in West London, where they have dealt with local councils to help people get access to Housing Benefit and with the Canal and River Trust to help stop people becoming homeless.

Another problem that has faced the boating community recently has been crime. Particularly in East London, there have been concentrated outbreaks of burglaries, towpath muggings and assaults. People have been robbed in their homes, and a cyclist was seriously injured when drunks tied a rope at head height across the towpath. Boats have been seen as easy targets by criminals, as they are often not very secure and may be left unattended for long periods. The emergency services tend not to be familiar with the layout of the canal network, which means they find it difficult to respond to reports of crimes.

London Boaters, through its full-time Community Organiser, has worked to involve the police and local councils to make them aware of the particular problems faced by boaters, and to educate boaters about how best to protect their homes and warn them about particular problems. One result of this has been that the police have set up a specialist team, Project Kraken, with particular knowledge of the canals around London. We have also recently started handing out whistles to boaters in the area to warn others and ward off intruders.

One sign of the growing complexity of the liveaboard community is the number of people using boats as a place of work. Virtually all boaters are supplied with fuel, whether that be coal, diesel or gas, by a small group of traders who continue to operate working boats on the canal network. In recent years, though, both the number and range of trading boats has increased dramatically.

In London alone, there is a bookshop, several boats selling clothing, including hats and vintage clothing, a variety of cafes and restaurant boats offering such delights as organic sandwiches, vegan cakes, ice cream and hot dogs. Entertainment is well catered for, too. The roofs of boats make an ideal stage for musicians, and there is one barge that has been converted to work as a floating circus. Together with what could be London's first floating herbal apothecary for 350 years, they make up a really vibrant community of water borne traders.

During the Olympics, official floating markets were set up. These attracted the whole range of local traders, along with many from further afield and many others who just decided to have a go. Since then, groups of trading boats have been a regular sight at most of London's most popular towpath locations, providing a varied, and constantly changing, attraction to visitors.

Stonebridge

An exciting prospect for boaters in the London area is a community centre next to the canal in Tottenham. The area suffers from high levels of crime and has always been difficult to manage. Its owners, the Canal and River Trust, are looking for a group to take over the running of this building, and we have some really interesting proposals for projects that we, along with some other community groups, can run there.

For example, the centre does not have mains sewerage, and pumping the cess pit is one of the main running costs. But there is unused space next to the building that we hope could be used to house a reed bed, which could reduce both the waste we produce and the cost of running the building.

We have already run a community café there, which made a tremendous difference to the area. Just having a place for people to meet has made the atmosphere much more friendly and inviting. We have also agreed for a mooring to be made available for a boater to work as a caretaker. Visitors have made all sorts of suggestions for activities we could run from there. Many of these have come from outside groups, providing us with opportunities to work in conjunction with other local community groups. And by having a presence there, we have found many ways we can run the

The community centre at Stonebridge Lock in Tottenham

centre more efficiently, saving money for its owners and reducing our costs. Perhaps most importantly, we think the café has a real chance of covering the running costs of the building.

In the future, we are hoping to provide a range of services for the boating community. Most important of these is a mail service. People living on a boat, particularly those without a permanent mooring, almost always struggle to get mail delivered reliably and this is something that will encourage people to make more use of the centre. Also, the lack of a land address is the cause of many kinds of social exclusion boaters face. On the back of the mail service, we hope to run a launderette. And we want to set up a bulk food buying scheme in conjunction with the café.

As the size of the liveaboard community has grown, so has the number of families bringing up children on board. Some of those families have already started organising their own groups, and the prospect of having a community centre we can use expands the possibilities open to them in the future.

All these projects will make the boating community more self-reliant and encourage more people to put their own plans into action. This is an exciting time for boaters in London, as we make the transition from a group of nomadic individuals to a fully-fledged community using its own resources to support itself.

Tony Smetham
has been an active member of London Boaters which is becoming a pioneer of community-based provision of services and facilities for boaters (e.g. moorings, boaters' credit union). Tony believes that this could serve as a template for use in other areas.

Who builds the house?

JENNY PICKERILL

*Most houses in low impact developments in Britain are built by men.
Jenny explores why this matters and describes some ways in which
women have started to reclaim the task of building their own homes.*

Gender is just one form of difference between us;
we also differentiate ourselves by race, class,
sexuality, size, and many other markers. But
when it comes to examining how houses are built in
low impact developments, the biggest divide is around
gender. Despite the feminist movement, significant
gains in equality between genders in the last century,
and the fact that low impact developments tend to
be politically left and liberal, the gender politics of
building often go ignored.

Men dominate eco-building through a mixture of blatant
and subtle ways, though, as with all generalisations
there are important exceptions. This chapter is not a
tirade against men, rather it explores how both men and
women involved in low impact developments struggle
to overcome gender as a form of division, and how this
has consequences for both genders. By ignoring gender as an issue we are potentially excluding a wealth
of knowledge and labour from eco-building. Gender
should not be a barrier to being a builder, but neither
can it be ignored. Exploring gender requires us to look
at the social aspects of housing as being as important
as the physical structure, and thus including more
women might also change how our homes are built.

I have been researching and working with low impact
developments and eco-communities for the last dec-

Amy at her house

ade.[1] In particular I conducted a research project comparing British eco-communities with those in Spain, Thailand, Argentina and the USA, visiting 30 different communities overall. My interest is in how eco-houses get built, the decisions, choices and dilemmas involved, the costs (social and emotional as well as economic), the compromises, and how the completed house is lived in, works and functions. In other words, the social practices through which eco-houses are built and lived in. This approach is vital in order to understand why we do not have more eco-houses. We already have the knowledge, technology, materials, built exemplars and often the finance, and yet few people choose to build, or even live in, an eco-house. If we can examine what drives those people who do build low impact developments and how their choices are made, then we would be better able to encourage others to do the same.

A brief history of women building houses
There are some interesting historical examples of women being actively involved in house building. In the Pueblos of New Mexico (USA) indigenous women led house building. Although the men erected the main timbers, women did everything else, including being responsible for physical maintenance of the buildings.[2] In the USA in the 1970s the feminist movement fought to challenge the mainstream ways of building houses

and instead designed kitchenless houses as a way to free women from their domestic burden.[3] At the same time many eco-communities emerged in that era with increasing numbers of women trained as carpenters, and builders, and women were heavily involved in construction of their own homes.

Assumptions about women

Throughout my travels through many eco-communities it was rare to meet a female eco-builder. Even so, when I raised the issue of gender many people denied there was a problem, instead asserting that the lack of women on build projects was a result of women's personal choice. Gender exclusion today is rarely blatant; it tends to rely on often quite subtle assumptions made about women's minds, bodies and roles in society, which are then reinforced by both men and women repeating and performing those roles. People might not

Glass brick making

even realise that they are being sexist in voicing these assumptions, and women might not believe that their 'personal choices' are influenced by such assumptions. Yet however hard we try we are very often influenced by what those around us say, do and expect of us, and thus naming those expectations and assumptions has been an important part of the feminist movement. This focus on gender, however, is complicated by emerging understandings of transgendered and intersexed people who do not fit the rigid binary distinctions of women/ men and thus transgress gender norms. So in using the terms men/ women I am simplifying the current debates.

Alex at her house

Building zome

For example, in western society it has long been assumed that a woman's role is primarily to have and raise a family and, in so doing, to spend much of her time in the home doing domestic chores (such as cleaning, childcare and food production). Thus a woman becomes stereotyped as a 'homemaker'.[4] Interestingly in this context women make homes, but it is men who build them. These assumptions are evident when women seek to do different things such as have demanding careers, choose not to have children, take up risky sports such as mountaineering, or work in traditionally male dominated fields such as engineering or architecture. The lack of women on the boards of top companies reflects the underlying assumptions in society that women are not equal to men.

There are those who believe these differences between genders are biological, that women are different not just in bodily form but also in brain chemistry, thinking skills and spatial abilities.[5] These views, however, are convenient ways in which women can be constrained to roles which suit a patriarchal society. Instead, feminists have long argued that gender is a social category with which various stereotypes tend to be associated. Thus women are constructed to be feminine, caring, creative, and emotional. Yet, as many men also identify with these character traits, it becomes possible to understand gender as a spectrum and therefore women as being no less good at being scientific, rational, strong or careerist than men. Rather, both men and women become constrained by society's expectations and stereotypes.

Assumptions about building
These assumptions influence justifications as to why women's minds, bodies and roles in society stop them from being good at eco-building. A popular opinion amongst builders I interviewed was that women are not as physically strong or able as men and because building is primarily about strength women would be limited in what they could do. This assumption is misleading in three ways. First, women are not necessarily weaker than men; there is a huge diversity in our body types and capabilities, and such assumptions do a disservice to both strong women and men who have a weaker body. Second, if building requires strength there are a number of ways to make this navigable to those less strong, such as using smaller block sizes or working in teams. Many such changes have already been made in recent years to comply with health and safety requirements. Finally, strength is rarely the most important skill in building;

The physical aspect of building is to me a small aspect. There's so much you have to do right. You have to really pay attention to what you're doing, and those details or just making things plumb or level, you really have to think ahead in order to integrate what's going to come later and later and later with what you're doing now... It takes so much more than just your brute force, and it's a lot more important, that thinking stuff.
Amanda Bramble
Ampersand Sustainable Learning Center,
New Mexico, USA

Similar assumptions are made about women's mental capabilities. These tend to identify women as naturally more creative, but less scientific than men. Consequently women's artistic input is welcomed, but their views on structural design are not. These assumptions can be expressed in quite subtle ways, which might not immediately appear sexist or derogatory;

I feel as if it's more accessible to more people if it's not a science but an art, and natural building sometimes, often, feels more of an art to me than a science.
Gregory Crawford
Panya Project, Thailand

For women at Panya Project, however, these sentiments were restrictive in determining who could do what on a build project;

> *There was definitely a more feminine presence in the creative aspect; men seemed quite happy to let women somewhat direct the artistic side of things, but when it comes to talking practically they're a little bit challenged. There needs to be a bit more of men coming in and being creative. There are a lot of creative men that live here and come through here, and there are a lot of practical women who come through too. It is allowing both sides to acknowledge that.*
>
> Shelley
> Panya Project, Thailand

Finally, different roles in society are often aligned with different genders. These stereotypes of what men and women do can be surprisingly entrenched, making them hard to challenge. For example, childcare is still, in the main, associated with women, while manual occupations such as mining or building tend to be viewed as best suited to men. Feminists have been challenging these stereotypes for centuries and yet they still remain. The problem in low impact developments is that despite being politically alternative in many ways these stereotypes still influence the division of labour within them and how building is perceived by others. Even when construction has been a joint effort,

the contribution of women gets undervalued. Often women do the support work for a build – collecting build materials, cleaning, planting, cooking for volunteers, etc – but because this is less visible than the men's contribution it gets overlooked. Instead, houses become 'Simon's house' or 'Tony's house'. This also has consequences for men. For example, in Green Hills (UK) the men had to take over the gardening business for a while as both the women were heavily pregnant. One of the men realised that actually he loved gardening more than building (which he had taken on by default for many years), and has ever since been far more hands-on in the garden.

Women building houses
Despite gender being largely ignored as an issue in low impact developments there are pockets of excellent examples of women building and teaching others to.

These should be celebrated, and by learning from their approach we can encourage more gender equality.

Several projects deliberately focus on the importance of the body in building, but rather than discussing strength as a key attribute, they teach that all builders need to re-learn how to use their whole body in building. This is most obvious in natural building where builders such as Paulina Wojciechowska of Earth Hands and Houses teach how to use our bodies in making and using earth plasters. Others, such as Shay Salomon (USA) and the Mud Girls (Canada) lead women-only builds as places women can feel comfortable in themselves to try things out, experiment and not be judged.[6]

Challenging the assumptions that others and women themselves make about women's mental capabilities is quite difficult. We need to identify and support leading female eco-builders such as Barbara Jones (Strawworks), Brenda Vale (The Autonomous House), Rachel Shiamh (Quiet Earth), Lydia Doleman (The Flying Hammer), Alix Henry (Henry Architects), Kirsten Jacobson (Earthship Biotecture) and Amanda Bramble (Ampersand Sustainable Learning Center) to name just a few. These women have already proved that gender is no barrier to being outstanding architects, builders and designers. At the same time we need to celebrate diversity in building practice. By questioning the emphasis on strength we can instead stress the importance of other practices, like communication and listening, as being central to successful building. This is not to reject that certain engineering principles are best to follow, but we should acknowledge that there are multiple ways to build a good house.

Finally, in trying to change the broader societal expectations of what men and women do, we need to embrace gender as a form of diversity but not as a division of labour. We need to create space for women to build and to acknowledge the work that many women already do on build sites. This is about making women's contributions visible and valuing them in the language we use to describe houses. It is also about encouraging women to be whatever they wish, to learn from the knowledge we already have, but also to be free to make mistakes and have the space to learn from doing.

Next steps
There are several steps we could take to get more women building eco-houses:

- Facilitate builders of all genders to reflect and discuss their assumptions and views. This should not be about blaming men for women's limited involvement. Rather, change requires all participants to acknowledge there is a problem and collectively identify solutions.

- Educate on how many existing assumptions are sexist and unnecessary, and illustrate how many women are expert eco-builders through sharing examples of their technical work.

- Facilitate and run women only building workshops through which to share skills, knowledge and examples.

- Support women only experimental space for building; a space which would enable women to experiment without being judged and to have the freedom to learn through doing.

- Establish women eco-build support groups as forums for sharing advice, stories and experiences.

Acknowledgements

This research was supported by a Winston Churchill Memorial Trust Travel Fellowship 2010 (http://www.wcmt.org.uk/).

Jenny Pickerill

works in the University of Leicester's Geography Department and lives in an eco-house. She can be contacted on j.pickerill@le.ac.uk

Notes

1   Pickerill, J and Maxey, L (2009) *Geographies of sustainability: Low Impact Developments and radical spaces of innovation*, Geography Compass, 3, 4, 1515-1539
2   Crews, C (2010) *Clay Culture: Plasters, Paints and Preservation.* Gourmet Adobe Press, New Mexico.
3   Hayden, D (1981) *The Grand Domestic Revolution: A History of Feminist Designs for American Homes, Neighborhoods, and Cities.* The MIT Press, London.
4   Blunt, A and Dowling, R (2006) *Home.* Routledge, London.
5   Hines, M (2004) *Brain Gender.* Oxford University Press, Oxford.
6   Salomon, S (2006) *Little House on a Small Planet: Simple Homes, Cozy Retreats and Energy Efficient Possibilities.* The Lyons Press, Guilford, Connecticut.

The Ecological Land Co-operative

SHAUN CHAMBERLIN

With echoes of the Land Settlement Association and County Council Smallholdings has the Ecological Land Co-operative started to crack development in the open countryside?

L and is (or should be) invaluable, perhaps even sacred. It is a place to live, a source for food, for water, for fuel, and for sustenance of almost every kind. Yet as Simon Fairlie put it, in Britain "nearly half the country is owned by 40,000 land millionaires, or 0.06 per cent of the population, while most of the rest of us spend half our working lives paying off the debt on a patch of land barely large enough to accommodate a dwelling and a washing line".

Meanwhile, land management choices have profound impacts on the UK's ecosystems and environment, and thus on our health, well-being and collective future. So it is of deep significance that while – in this country – supermarkets and housing estates find permission to build easy to come by, those who wish to use land to explore truly sustainable living are blocked and frustrated at every turn.

It is this sorry state of affairs that has given birth to the Reclaim the Fields movement and activist groups like Grow Heathrow and the Diggers 2012. Inspired by the example of Gerrard Winstanley's 17th Century Diggers, these peaceful, practical radicals have moved onto disused UK land in order to cultivate it, build dwellings and live in common "by the sweat of our brow".

In other words, they have asserted their right to simply exist on nature's bounty, seeking neither permission from anyone nor dominion over anyone; a right that they believe people should still share with the other animals. A right, indeed, that was enshrined in UK law in the 1217 Charter of the Forest. More recently, however, the strange young notion of owning exclusive rights to land has pushed back hard. Thus, as they fully expected – and as happened to their forebears – the Diggers 2012's crops have been torn up and they themselves have been hassled, moved on and in some cases arrested.

It might seem, then, that the efforts of these determined folk are being successfully repelled by 'the system', were it not for two crucial considerations – that they have history on their side, and that there is an enormous army surging at their backs. As we look around the world, we see them, from the likes of the 1.5m strong Landless Workers' Movement in Brazil and the vast international peasant's movement La Via Campesina, to the tens of thousands of Greek families deserting the cities to return to any land they can access and the immense – and apparently successful – land rights march across India earlier this year.

Plot A before development commenced

Meanwhile, closer to home, I see increasing numbers of my friends disillusioned and marginalised from the mainstream economy – ripped off by the banks, burdened with huge debts and struggling to find decent employment. As the inherently unsustainable financial economy continues to unravel, the people of England are not yet reaping the desperate consequences to the

extent that those of Greece or India are, but it is growing even here, and it will come heavily home to this dark heart of the financial empire soon enough. For many, 'austerity' is already biting hard.

Naturally, in such circumstances, we seek alternatives. Yet while some might wish to follow the example of those Greek families and earn a simple, honest life "by the sweat of our brow", rather than working frantically to earn 'a living' while paying off the debts incurred by a corrupt financial system, they are simply not being permitted to do so.

Absurd new laws which criminalise the likes of squatting and trespass are being passed. This is even against the wishes of the police forces and means that the police are being forced to step in on behalf of landowners. Meanwhile, ongoing political reform of planning policy is making it ever easier for corporations – and harder for families – to control land, leaving the courts obliged to prosecute those who wish to work to heal disused, neglected land instead of relying on state handouts to survive the vagaries of the employment market. The glaring injustice that has mobilised mass movements in the likes of Brazil and India is becoming ever more apparent here.

Thus I see the tide of history at the backs of the Diggers 2012, with their direct action the vanguard of an inevitable UK movement to reclaim the land under our feet from the 1% – or 0.06% – who would call it theirs.

What are we fighting for?
Yet, as with all influential movements for change in society, the activists cannot achieve much alone. Their essential direct action and willingness to put their bodies on the line powerfully expresses and demonstrates the ever-swelling public pressure. But if that pressure is to lead to a better society (rather than simply widespread frustration and anger) we also need positive lifestyle examples for law-abiding citizens to follow, complemented by the slow work of developing alternative legal and organisational forms that allow land to meet the pressing needs of the people.

With the UK population having swelled by 4 million over the past decade, it becomes ever more pertinent that the uniform, large-scale, mechanised agriculture produced by consolidated land ownership has long been known to produce far less food per acre than smaller holdings (let's not even mention the relative productivity of grouse moors or golf courses!).

This may seem counter-intuitive as it is common knowledge that many smaller farms have been forced out of business due to being economically uncompetitive. But, in fact, it is not a lack of productivity that causes small farms to suffer in our modern economy. Their first problem is that although they can produce substantially more food per acre, the big farms can produce more of a given monoculture crop per acre, which suits the large-scale centralised buyers (those same supermarkets who reportedly receive planning permission for a new UK store every working day of the year).

The greater challenge facing smallholders, however, is that their higher productivity per acre relies on higher employment. Just as the most productive parts of large farms famously tend to be the farmers' gardens, where more time and attention is lavished on each plant among a diverse crop, smallholdings rely on careful human attention, which can be a major expense. Large-scale mechanised farms, on the other hand, have echoed other industries in taking advantage of fuel prices over recent decades to replace human care with cheap fossil energy, standardisation and monoculture. Yet with finite fossil fuel supplies depleting and oil prices having tripled over the past decade, the balance is shifting.

Smallholdings and horticulture, then, offer a crucial contribution towards higher employment, a reliable, home-grown food supply for the UK (rising energy prices are also a threat to cheap imports) and a diverse and thus more ecologically healthy countryside. Considering this alongside our government's calls for more consumption of fresh fruit and vegetables (and less dependence on state handouts) it is perhaps unsurprising to learn of the set up of a government-funded Land Settlement Association to provide over a thousand 5 acre smallholdings, and to train unemployed workers in the skills required to manage them.

Unfortunately though, this welcome initiative was launched in 1934, and was wound up – with all the holdings privatised – in 1983, by which point the LSA was producing around 40% of English home grown salad crops. The subsidies (and research funding) in place today are far more supportive of big agribusiness than of any modern equivalent of the LSA, but it

Installation of the well

nevertheless provides an inspiring, practical example of what could be done.

Back in the 1930s the primary motivation for supporting smallholdings in this way was to provide jobs for the unemployed, but the need for similar provision is perhaps more acute than ever today in the face of our profound environmental crisis. Industrialised agriculture is a major contributor to climate destabilisation, soil depletion and numerous other problems, while smallholdings provide an ideal context for diverse, low-carbon, localised lifestyles that could provide a desperately needed model for true sustainability.

Meanwhile, UK agriculture is suffering from a lack of new blood – the average age of a UK farm holder is now 58 – since private farms are now generally far too large for would-be new farmers to afford, and the 'County Farms' made available to new entrants by local authorities (around 40% of which are under 50 acres in size) are gradually being sold off as the austerity funding cuts bite ever harder.

Fair to say, then, that productive low-impact land use could represent a key response to many of our most pressing social, economic and ecological problems. And, as the popularity of *Diggers and Dreamers* attests, there is also a great appetite for the diverse lifestyles they could provide. Yet extortionate land prices and the intricate absurdities of the planning permission system combine to make the simple aim of living on and working a piece of land seem an unattainable dream for most of us.

This is why in 2012 I agreed to become a director of an organisation called the Ecological Land Co-operative, which exists to support those wishing to establish small-scale ecological businesses and smallholdings in overcoming these two great barriers to land access.

The Ecological Land Co-operative

The Eco Land Co-op emerged from energetic discussions in the spring of 2005 between members of Chapter 7, the ecological planning consultancy; Radical Routes, a secondary co-operative of co-operatives working for social change; Somerset Co-operative Services, a co-op development body; and farms and eco-communities like Landmatters, Lammas, Highbury Farm and Five Penny Farm.

They were yearning for a vibrant, living countryside in which humans flourish alongside our cherished landscapes and natural biodiversity, with small land-based enterprises providing meaningful employment while allowing residents to be rooted in rural communities and play a crucial role in ensuring food and energy sovereignty. They were longing for a proliferation of happy rural lifestyles, helping to maintain traditional skills and improve ecological literacy while providing access to local, sustainable crafts and food, as well as educational opportunities for urban visitors.

Roundwood, timber-framed communal barn

And, as so often when such breathy, passionate desires are unleashed, a child was eventually born...

The basic idea of the Co-operative is that it buys land that has been, or is at risk of being, intensively managed, then uses its expertise and experience to oversee the process of securing planning permission for low-impact residences on site. Once this is achieved, the land is made available at an affordable price to people that have the skills to manage it ecologically but who could not otherwise afford to do so. The money received when the new residents buy their land is then used to purchase another intensively managed site, where the same process can begin, allowing more land to be 'rescued' from industrialised agriculture.

Prospective residents of a piece of land are only asked to buy in once planning permission for their homes is secured, but they do have to sign up to a strict management plan which requires that the land is always managed so as to maintain and enhance habitats, species diversity and landscape quality, and to facilitate the provision of low-impact livelihoods. There are also conditions stipulating that if they ever want to sell up and move on, the land must be sold on at an affordable price, so that the land is never priced out of reach. Beyond that, the land will be theirs to run as they see fit.

That was the idea. How about the reality?

Well, as an informal group, the Eco Land Co-op received some early funding from the Co-operative Group in the South West for scoping and feasibility work, and at later stages in our development from the Co-operative Fund, Business Link and the Polden-Puckham Charitable Foundation. These helped the Co-op find its feet and put basic organisational structures in place.

In 2009 we sold community shares to finance the purchase of our first land, a 22-acre site on the Devon/Somerset border which we christened Greenham Reach. We have divided this land into three plots, in order to allow each of three 'clustered' smallholdings the independence to build their own dwelling and manage their land as they wish, while also enjoying the benefits of a small community for tool-sharing, sociability, mutual support etc. Accordingly, we also plan to provide some infrastructure to be shared between the three smallholdings – a timber barn with solar PV array and rainwater collection; improved access; a biological waste water treatment system and internal pathways linking the plots.

Installation of rainwater catchment system

Unfortunately, shortly after our land purchase, the setbacks began – firstly in working with a planning agent who appears to have misled us and who failed to submit valid planning applications on our behalf on three separate occasions. This depressing episode set the project back by around a year, but we will definitely be wiser next time around.

Our original hopes to secure planning permission for the site before inviting applications from potential plotholders were also thwarted, as the District Council informed us that they wanted to see individual business plans from the prospective residents before they would consider granting permission. Accordingly, we advertised and went through a selection process in 2011, selecting from the applicants on a number of criteria including their farming and horticultural experience, vision and plans for the land, experience of low impact living and connection with the locality.

Crowdfunding and community financing also allowed us to produce the *Small is Successful* report at this time, examining eight existing smallholdings with land-based businesses on ten acres or less. These documented examples demonstrate that economically viable and highly sustainable land based livelihoods can be created on this scale, without any need for the subsidies on which large farms so often rely. The Research Council UK showcased *Small is Successful* as one of a hundred pieces of UK research "that will

Installation of sand and gravel filter for producing drinking water

have a profound effect on our future", and we were also invited to present our message to the All Party Parliamentary Group for Agroecology at the House of Commons, all of which helped support our case for the viability and importance of small-scale holdings.

Together with our new intended plotholders, we then submitted the full applications for the three plots at the end of 2011, doing it ourselves this time. They ran to over 400 pages of careful documentation, and more than sixty letters of support were also received by the Council, including from experienced organic smallholders; local residents; the Soil Association; the Transition Network; Sustrans; Colin Tudge's Campaign for Real Farming; Food Policy Professor Tim Lang and other academics; three MPs and even the Scottish Crofting Federation. We also won recommendations for approval from both the local Parish Council and the planning officers who spent the best part of a year carefully going through our applications, and a particularly heartening letter came from a planner of over 30 years' experience, who described our work as "by some way the most carefully prepared applications for either an agricultural and/or low impact dwelling I have considered".

Nonetheless, in common with other similar low-impact proposals, in June 2012 we attended a hearing to witness the rejection of our applications by the councillors on Mid Devon District Council's planning committee.

The vote for rejection was based on their vague statements that smallholdings are not "serious farming", that the business plans – despite being carefully reviewed by a number of agricultural experts – "do not stack up" and that off-grid renewables are "not practical" (in part because apparently "there isn't enough wind on the site for PV"). The official reasons for refusal, drafted over a tea break after the vote was taken, reflected the principal concern about our application:

> *"If granted, based upon the supporting information submitted, the proposal would set a precedent for further dwellings, in association with permaculture and agroforestry proposals, in the countryside which the Local Planning Authority would find hard to resist."*

However, believing our case to be a strong one, we proceeded to an appeal inquiry (heard in January 2013) and received the Inspector's verdict in April 2013 with the news we had all been working and hoping for. She granted permission, indicating that she valued both the co-operative model we have developed and the research and monitoring of changes in biodiversity, soil carbon and productivity which will be delivered alongside the smallholdings, while noting that the Council had failed to have regard for our:

> *"aims of addressing the need to reduce the negative impacts of conventional farming and globalised food distribution...*
>
> *I accept that the labour-intensive nature of such practices, necessary to ensure that a sustainable livelihood could be developed without resort to agro-chemicals and the reliance on fossil fuels, would require the worker's presence and involvement to such an extent that the need could only be met by living on-site...*
>
> *Provided that proposals for other dwellings associated with permaculture and agroforestry complied with the relevant policies, it is not clear to me why the Council would consider encouragement for them to be undesirable."*

What next?
All in all, it has been a long struggle since those idealistic conversations seven years ago, but we are now closing in on the great satisfaction of having something simple and solid to show for our efforts – smallholders

living on and working the land who would otherwise have been unable to do so. At the time of writing it is only a fortnight since the Inspector's decision, but we are already working hard to get the smallholdings at Greenham Reach up-and-running as soon as possible.

It will be a small beginning, perhaps, but we fully intend to apply the invaluable experience gained to date by finding further suitable land to make available in future. The Inspector's decision also opens up the possibility that in future we may be able to seek planning permission for future sites before having to involve tenants, as we had originally intended. We dare to dream that it could be the start of a real solution to the thorny problem of land access here in the UK.

We have also begun a second research project, collaborating with others in the movement to produce a resource establishing both the current state of ecological farming in the UK – providing a single point of information on who is doing what and where, what acreages, to what markets, etc – and the current state of research into such agriculture.

I see this work as supporting and strengthening the wider movement to reclaim land from the ecologically destructive, market-driven mainstream of conventional land use. Or, if that sounds a little grand, perhaps I can borrow from one who speaks more plainly? In the words of a U.S. farmer quoted in Colin Tudge's So Shall We Reap:

Installing off-grid photovoltaic panels on the communal barn

Topping-out of the communal compost toilet

"I just want to farm well. I don't want to compete with anybody."

In this world of frantic capitalism, there is a radical thought if ever I heard one.

It is a thought that inspires me. I feel more and more that the people the world needs most right now are not campaigners or activists, but such people who simply wish to live in relationship with a piece of land in a healing, productive and ecologically nurturing way. There is no shortage of them, and we should be making it as easy as possible for them to access land, without forcing them to launch political campaigns or planning permission battles in order to do so.

Perhaps that vast and diverse movement – from the Diggers 2012 and La Via Campesina to Diggers and Dreamers and the Eco Land Co-op – in truth has but one simple aim. To safeguard the quiet dignity of that farmer, and the billions like him.

Shaun Chamberlin
became a director of the ELC in 2012. He has also been involved with the Transition Network since its inception, co-founding Transition Town Kingston and authoring the movement's second book, *The Transition Timeline* (Green Books, 2009). He writes at: www.darkoptimism.org

- To find out more, take a look at the website: http://ecologicalland.coop/ or follow us on Twitter: @EcoLandCoop

- You can also join ELC mailing list by emailing: zoe@ecologicalland.coop

- Any offers of time or assistance are also greatly appreciated, to the same email address.

What is stopping low impact going mainstream?

SIMON FAIRLIE

Low-impacters are a pretty inventive lot so why is it that so few examples of LID have actually happened?

In 1995, when I first began writing about Low Impact Development (LID), it was hard to find many actual examples in the UK. There were a couple of bender camps, Kings Hill and Tinkers' Bubble; there were the lowland crofting sites in Scotland (that were not particularly low impact); there were smallholders living in caravans and shacks; and, thankfully, there was Hockerton Housing Project.

Hockerton consists of a terrace of five earth-sheltered eco-homes built on 20 acres of land on the outskirts of a Nottinghamshire village. Even though it was outside the development area, the project had been given planning permission in 1994. The planning authority recommendation for approval stated:

> *"If this was a simple application for a housing scheme in the countryside it would not be at all acceptable... In this exceptional case there is a justification because the applicants have outlined in some detail how the whole development would interact and go some way towards creating a sustainable development."*

Such a decision is permitted by Section 54A of the Town and Country Planning Act which states that "determination shall be made in accordance with the development plan, unless material considerations indicate otherwise" the material considerations in this case being sustainability. Hockerton exemplified the principle that

"LID is development that, by virtue of its low or benign environmental impact, may be allowed in locations where conventional development is not permitted."[1]

It was a prize example, since these were no hippie hovels, but pukka houses, the sort of place your mother would find comfortable and your local MP would applaud. In 1998 it was opened by the then Minister for Construction, Nick Raynsford.

Now, 18 years later, there are hundreds of examples of low impact development: yurts and wooden shacks have proliferated, benders have become more grandiose, and various other kinds of alternative housing have arrived on the scene: straw bale houses, "hobbit houses", turf-roofed roundhouses and so on. Most of these have been given planning permission retrospectively, either because they are associated with agricultural or forestry projects that provide a justification for living on site, or else because they remained undiscovered long enough to become immune from enforcement (the four-year and ten-year rules).

But it is hard to find any replicas of the Hockerton experiment. There are plenty of one-off eco-houses and "passivhausen"; there are one or two cohousing projects, such as Forgebank, constructed on an old mill site near Lancaster; there are a few affordable housing projects on "rural exception sites" whose design is influenced by the low impact movement. But I know of no other case where permission has been given in advance for a group of houses on a rural site outside the development zone on the grounds that, despite being in conflict with the development plan, the project is low impact and sustainable.

This is not for lack of trying, nor is it for lack of demand. From the enquiries that come to Chapter 7, it is clear that there is a huge demand for low impact housing which is not tied to agricultural or forestry livelihoods, but that nonetheless provides people with access to a modest area of land for food and energy production, and for home-based businesses. The genuine back-to-the-land peasants are in a minority, compared to the number of people who simply want to "downsize". Quite a few of these well-intentioned downsizers buy a few acres of land and try to go down the agricultural worker's dwelling route, on the basis of a level of self-sufficiency that could be less stressfully achieved in a house on the edge of a village with a large garden.

The purpose of the planning system, one might reasonably suppose, is to provide for people's needs whilst ensuring that the local and wider environments and other people's amenity are protected. It would not be that hard to devise a set of policies that met downsizers' needs by allowing small clusters of low impact ecohomes with access to workshops and agricultural land to be built on the edge of settlements, in much the same way that affordable housing has been permitted through the rural exception sites policy.

Such a policy would expect applicants to meet a number of criteria relating to the use of local and renewable building materials, reliance on renewable and passive solar energy, the provision of a car pool, the management of wastes and so on. It would require the involvement of an organisation, such as a cohousing group, a co-op or a development trust, to ensure that these standards were adhered to over changes of ownership and occupation. In order to ensure that the agricultural land did not end up as oversized suburban gardens or wasteland, it would be advisable to have it managed as a common resource that could be rented in the form of allotments or paddocks to any residents who needed to use it at any given time.

And, if deemed appropriate, the development could be maintained indefinitely as affordable housing through a legal agreement.

All of this would be quite do-able through planning policies and legal mechanisms that would not be that different to those that already exist for affordable housing, but no local authority has done it. Planners know only too well that there is huge pressure from people wanting to move to the country, but rather than work out how to channel that desire into low impact, mixed use developments that bring life back into rural settlements, they try to suppress it as though there was something warped and antisocial about wanting a rural lifestyle.

This allergic reaction to rural resettlement has been evident in the reaction to the new Low Impact Development policy that has been introduced in Wales, entitled One Planet Development (OPD). This policy allows developments which facilitate a significant reduction in ecological footprint to take place in locations where conventional development might not normally be allowed, and hence on sites that are affordable.

The original policy, in the 2010 Welsh planning guidance for the countryside, TAN 6, states quite clearly that "One Planet Developments may be located within or adjacent to existing settlements, or be situated in the open countryside." But when the Practice Guide for One Planet Development was published in 2012, it focused entirely on OPDs in the open countryside, stipulating (quite rightly) that applicants wishing to reside on land in the open countryside away from any settlement needed to be making a substantial proportion of their living from their land.

There was not a word in this document, or any other, explaining how people who make their living as a farrier, a rural nurse, a village schoolteacher or a jobbing gardener, for example, should go about applying for a One Planet Development within or on the edge of a settlement, nor does there appear to be any intention to produce one. All the attention so far has been focussed on the aspirations of a minority of hard-core would-be peasants, while the needs of the vast majority of people who do not earn their living from small-scale agriculture have been systematically ignored. Every single application for OPD to date has been for a land-based holding in the open countryside. The One Planet Development policy has effectively been marginalised to what many people view as a hippie backwater, and there are plenty of policymakers who would be happy to see it stay there, in the hope that it will eventually fade away through its own irrelevance.

In any case it is arguable that the One Planet Development policy actually makes it harder rather than easier for land-based LIDs to get permission, since it is so prescriptive. The high profile Lammas project, involving a cluster of nine smallholdings in Pembrokeshire, was given permission (at appeal) because its painstakingly detailed application addressed every single one of these prescriptions. But aside from that, the success rate of applications has not been brilliant, and as of June 2013, the three most recent applications have all been dismissed at appeal.

In England there is no low impact policy to compare with One Planet Development, but most competent low impact smallholdings manage to acquire permission, usually at appeal, through a slightly fudged interpretation of the standard agricultural and forestry workers policy. Furthermore, most land-based low impact communities manage to acquire permission even though there is no policy to cover them. Indeed it is precisely because they do not fit neatly into policy that communities such as Kings Hill and Tinkers' Bubble in Somerset, and Land Matters and Steward Wood in Devon have managed to get permission. In the absence of a targeted policy, inspectors are obliged to assess each application on its merits, and in each of the above four cases an Inspector found that there was sufficient merit to justify giving permission.

In principle there is no reason why this approach could not be used by a mixed use co-housing project on the lines proposed at the beginning of this article. Locate a piece of land appropriately sited on the edge of a village with decent facilities, but outside the area allocated for development, and hence affordable. Then make a detailed outline application for low impact housing showing how, as at Hockerton, the scheme's sustainable and low impact attributes together with its social and economic benefits, constitute material considerations that outweigh the fact that it does not comply with housing land allocation policy. Be ready to see it refused by the local authority, but hope for an enlightened Inspector at appeal.

Since Hockerton there have been several projects that have attempted to go down this route, but none of them have materialised. There are four main reasons for this.

1   Such a scheme needs to be spearheaded by someone with boundless commitment, optimism, persistence, and an understanding of how the planning system works, and people like that are hard to find. The Plotgate project in Barton St David, Somerset, where low impact impresario Chris Black has bought 23 acres of land on the edge of a village helpfully sited between a horseshoe factory and an abandoned scrapyard, has been struggling for about five years largely because no one has come forward capable of filling this role.

2   The process of applying is usually so long and tortuous that it is hard to find people who will stay the course. Just when you think you are getting somewhere, the authorities come up with some other bureaucratic obstacle that sets everything back another few months. Professional developers are used to having to wait five years or longer to secure permission on land they have earmarked. If their architect or planning consultant decides to emigrate to New Zealand, that doesn't matter, they just employ another. But individuals seeking a home who join a prospective housing scheme usually can't afford to wait five years. As time drags on they become impatient and lose enthusiasm, or some other opportunity crops up and they drop out, taking their money with them. If professional help is employed the

project starts to become increasingly expensive. Eventually the whole thing fizzles out.

3   Bureaucratic requirements increase the cost of the scheme to the point where it no longer is an affordable or attractive proposition. Local authority officials of various denominations typically pile on requirements in the form of building regulations, design and access requirements, fire regulations, health and safety obligations and so on, with the result that a self-built house that might initially have cost £20,000 or £30,000 gradually doubles or triples in cost. This was one of the factors that put paid to the Future Roots project which a few years ago had local authority backing for a housing scheme near Langport, Somerset. One of the requirements, which many of the prospective residents did not want, was for a tarmac road running through the sloping site, wide enough to enable fire engines to enter.

4   Many low impact self-builders do not have a sufficiently clear idea of what they want to be able put in a detailed planning proposal. They prefer to build organically, starting small and adapting the design and expanding the building to suit circumstances and the availability of materials. That is "how buildings learn", as Stewart Brand so brilliantly illustrated in his book of the same name.[2]

All of these above problems can be circumvented by one change of tactic. Move on and start building first and apply for permission retrospectively. That is what Kings Hill, Tinkers' Bubble, Land Matters and Steward Wood all did, and in every case it worked. As Tinker's Bubble's patriarch, Mike Zair, used to remark, "it is easier to obtain forgiveness than permission". The problem with this approach is that it is high risk – or at least appears to be – and so not attractive to people who want to invest their life savings in a new home, or sell their existing property in order to build an eco-house. People who are prepared to take the risk move on in benders, yurts, caravans and modest wooden shacks, and so, by definition, are not mainstream.

The National Planning Policy Framework
It would be good to find a way out of this impasse, not least because the time seems to be right for putting forward such proposals. The planning system is in a

state of upheaval, as a result of the government having withdrawn over 1,000 pages of planning guidance, and replaced them with the 50-page National Planning Policy Framework (NPPF). Much of this framework consists of ill-defined platitudes, but there are one or two elements in it which could help to make low impact development more acceptable.

The first is the advice, in paragraph 50 that

"LPAs [local planning authorities] should plan for a mix of housing based on... the needs of different groups in the community such as... people wishing to build their own homes."

This, I am fairly certain, is the first time that self-build has ever been mentioned in national planning guidance (even though it constitutes about eight per cent of all housing in the country). True, there is nothing here to say that self-builders should have access to anything other than building plots on allocated development land at sky-high prices. But it does suggest that if the people interested in self-build within any local authority formed a group, and gave themselves a name such as Barsetshire Self-Builders, then the planning authority would be under pressure to work with them, and hopefully be persuaded to insert favourable policies into the local plan.

The other change that is helpful relates to the abandonment of the concept of "open countryside". Three successive generations of planning guidance (issued in 1992, 1997 and 2004) have stated that "building in the open countryside, away from existing settlements or from areas allocated for development in development plans, should be strictly controlled". In response to this somewhat ambiguous phrasing, planners have typically chosen to define as open countryside "the area outside the settlement boundaries of those towns and villages shown on the proposals map. All other settlements or communities are therefore considered for planning purposes to be part of the open countryside."[3] You can be in the middle of a village and still be in the "open countryside."

Not only has the statement about development in the open countryside being strictly controlled been dropped, but the term "open countryside" doesn't occur anywhere in the NPPF (though it does appear in the governments' new planning guidance for gypsies and travellers). Instead, paragraph 55 of the NPPF states that "local planning authorities should avoid new isolated homes in the countryside, unless there are special circumstances" (for example the need for a rural worker to live on site, the reuse of disused buildings or the exceptional quality of the design).

This suggests that housing on the edge of villages, where it is obviously not "isolated" should be looked on favourably if it conforms with other policies in the NPPF, notably the advice, also in paragraph 55 that "to promote sustainable development in rural areas, housing should be located where it will enhance or maintain the vitality of rural communities". There has already been one appeal where an earth-sheltered house was allowed on the edge of a village in Cornwall, because the inspector considered that it was not "isolated" but "at a perceived transition point between settlement and countryside"[4]. A word of warning however: it is possible that some local authority development plans will reintroduce the concept of "open countryside" and that this will not be seen to be in conflict with the NPPF, in which case the development plan will hold sway.

The moment is therefore a good one for pushing through a low impact, self-build, mixed use housing scheme, catering for the sort of people who do not aspire to keep goats and burn charcoal on a Welsh mountainside. Here is my recipe for how to go about it:

1 Get a group of like-minded people together who can advance a few thousand pounds apiece towards the scheme;

2   Found a local Self-Builders Group and start negotiating with planners (but don't believe everything they say). Submit input into your local council's development plan.

3   Locate and buy a suitable piece of land next to a village that is going for not much more than agricultural prices. If the scheme folds you can sell it again and get your money back.

4   Allocate an amount of money to employ someone to spearhead the planning application. This is money you won't get back.

5   Put in an application, and if refused:

6   Go to appeal

7   If you lose your appeal, you can manage the land from a distance for two years and then try again, or else cut your losses and sell the land.

The alternative is to move onto the land between action 4 and action 5 and install provisional structures that if necessary can be removed without too much loss of investment. Then proceed with the planning application and appeal with the added reassurance that forgiveness is easier to obtain than permission. That's the way that most people (with the exception of Hockerton) have done it up until now – but it's not really the mainstream way of doing things.

Simon Fairlie
runs Chapter 7, an organization that provides planning advice to smallholders and other low income people in the countryside. He is also editor of The Land magazine, and earns a living by selling scythes. He is the author of Low Impact Development: Planning and People in a Sustainable Countryside and Meat:A Benign Extravagance

Notes
1   Simon Fairlie, *Low Impact Development*, Jon Carpenter, second edition, 1996, p. xiv.
2   Stewart Brand, *How Buildings Learn*, Penguin 1995.
3   *Flintshire Local Planning Guidance Note No 10: New Housing in the Open Countryside*, 2006).
4   "Leedstown", appeal decision reference number: 2171912

Tony's Questions

TONY WRENCH

Some of those eternal questions that have still not been answered!

> Can you entrench an ethos of environmental sustainability in words? Would it do any good if you could?

> How do we get new people to understand the reasons for setting the community up – can we pass on an ethical framework that makes sense to new people and doesn't sound like the old timers trying to entrench their viewpoint?

> Do we need to agree on what we do about foxes, badgers, rats, mice, cats, dogs, slugs..., or not?

How can we get the next generation, either by birth or by joining later, to own the place and its customs? To feel their ideas are important and that they are just as responsible as anyone else?

How responsible am I for what children get taught, first hand by example or secondhand from 'teaching'?

How do you provide land and space for the next generation to build their own houses or hang out spaces?

How do you get people who had a bad experience at meetings to come to meetings? How do you prevent the community being run just by keen people who like meetings? (but may hate singing, woodsmoke and the dark)? How do you prevent resentments without requiring attendance at feelings meetings etc?

Who can be trusted with the finances?

Should anyone be allowed to join a community before sorting their stuff out first? If the answer to this is no, then who does the judging? Who judges the judges?

How do communities get rid of tyrants before they create a negative spiral taking years to climb out from?

All these issues are relevant to me as I look at intentional communities. They are relevant even if the communities don't want to be called intentional communities and prefer to have some guru or dead hero or religious bond or set of assumed or stated beliefs. They also apply to the wider society and have direct parallels with our attitudes to politics, politicians, bankers and international relations.

Tony Wrench
and his partner built their own eco-house using the principles of permaculture to give them a home with a 'one planet' ecological footprint and right livelihood. He also designed the house to be beautiful and comfortable, so that others might be inspired to do likewise. The rest is history.

"My Bit of Sky" by Gill Barron (http://ipaint.org.uk)

Resources

The following is a select list/contact details of recent publications and other reports related to low impact living communities

- BANG, Jan. *Ecovillages: A Practical Guide to Sustainable Communities.* Floris Books (2005) ISBN: 978-0863154805

- FAIRLIE, Simon. *Low Impact Development: Planning and People in a Sustainable Countryside* (2nd Revised edition). Jon Carpenter Publishing, (2009) ISBN: 978-1906067076 [The book that started a movement – a re-examination of Britain's planning system from the bottom up – from the point of view of the planned, rather than of the planner. A tool for those who wish to live on the land in a sustainable manner, and for planners and politicians who would like to make it possible for them to do so.]

- HEWITT, M and TELFER, K, *Earthships: Building a zero carbon future for homes.* IHS BRE Press, (2007) ISBN: 978-1860819728

- HUNT, S, *The Revolutionary Urbanism of Street Farm: Eco-Anarchism, Architecture and Alternative Technology in the 1970s.* Tangent Books, (2014) ISBN: 978-1906477448

- JACOB, J, *New Pioneers: The Back-to-the-Land Movement and the Search for a Sustainable Future.* Penn State University Press (2006) ISBN: 978-0271029894

- LAUGHTON, R, *Surviving and thriving on the land: How to use your time and energy to run a successful smallholding.* Green Books, Totnes, Devon, (2008) ISBN: 978-1900322287

- LAW, B, *The Woodland House.* Permanent Publications, East Meon, Hampshire, (2008) ISBN: 978-1856230445

- LAW, B, *The Woodland Way: A Permaculture Approach to Sustainable Woodland Management.* Permanent Publications, (2001) ISBN: 978-1856230094

- PICKERILL, Dr Jenny. *Low Impact communities in Britain.* University of Leicester, (2012) **http://naturalbuild.files.wordpress.com/2012/03/low-cost-low-impact-housing-2012-high-res.pdf**

- PICKERILL, Dr Jenny and MAXEY, Larch (eds). *Low Impact Development, The future in our hands.* University of Leicester Department of Geography, (2008) ISBN: 978-1-870474-36-8

- ROAF, S, *Ecohouse.* Architectural Press, London, (2007) ISBN: 978-0415526777

- SCHWARZ, W and SCHWARZ, D. *Living Lightly: Travels in post-consumer society.* Jon Carpenter Publishing, Oxfordshire, (1998) ISBN: 978-1897766446

- SUGDEN, Chrissie. *Grounds for Hope: Ways to live legally on cheap land in the UK.* Permanent Publications, (2011) Available as an e-book: http://www.green-shopping.co.uk/grounds-for-hope-ways-to-live-legally-on-cheap-land-in-the-uk.html

- WIMBUSH, Paul, *The Birth of an Ecovillage* FeedaRead.com, (2012) ISBN: 978-1781764923

- WRENCH, T, *Building a Low-Impact Roundhouse.* Permanent Publications, (2001) ISBN: 978-1856231749

- *Draft National Planning Policy Framework,* Department of Communities & Local Government, HMSO, (2011), ISBN: 978-1-4098-3048-1 [The Coalition Government's framework to encourage greater community participation in UK planning issues, while also helping to stimulate more house building and supply.]

- Ben Law (Ben supplies material and skills for construction, especially using round pole timber) **www.ben-law.co.uk**

- Brighton Earthship: **www.lowcarbon.co.uk/earthship-brighton**

- Chapter 7 **www.tlio.org.uk/chapter7**

- Down to Earth **www.downtoearthproject.org.uk**

- Eco-Hamlets **www.eco-hamlets.org.uk**

- Eco-Village Network **www..ecovillage.org**

- Green Building Blog **http://naturalbuild.wordpress.com** **www.jennypickerill.info**

- *The Land.* An occasional magazine about land rights written by and for people who believe that the roots of justice, freedom, social security and democracy lie not so much in access to money, or to the ballot box, as in access to land and its resources... "campaign peacefully for access to land, its resources and the decision-making processes affecting them, for everyone, irrespective of race, creed, age or gender." **www.thelandmagazine.org.uk**

- LILO – Low Impact Life Onboard. Group offering information about the eco-boating community in Britain, as well as the LILO Handbook. a

guide and resource manual to low impact life on board. Co-written by anyone who has something to contribute – whether it's personal experience, a tip on where to find eco-products or designs for a new biodiesel reactor.
www.lilo.org.uk

- *Living in the Future* is a DVD which follows the hugely successful internet mini-series on Lammas. This 60 minute documentary produced by Undercurrents looks at how life has been for the ecovillage pioneers as they have endeavoured to create a new lifestyle for themselves in West Wales. The film is both light-hearted and moving, funny and serious – but most importantly it takes a good look at the reality beyond the dream
www.livinginthefuture.org

- Low Impact Living initiative (LILI) LILI was founded in 2001 by two members of Redfield Community. The community itself was founded in 1978, and in 2001 had solar hot water, compost loos, straw-bale buildings, organic gardens, orchards, soft fruit, bees, sheep, chickens, natural paints, lime, wood stoves, and one member was experimenting with making biodiesel from waste cooking oil.
www.lowimpact.org

- Permaculture Magazine and Permanent Publications
www.permaculture.co.uk

- PlotGate Venture Co-operative and Community Land Trust. A co-operative exploring the appropriate use and development of the rural environment, to increase resilience in an uncertain world. On 23 acres of land in Somerset, they are practising and playing with enlightened agricultural principles to create an abundant, minimal input food system that is

able to meet their appetites, whilst enriching the ecological diversity of the land. People are a part of the ecology and they wish to create a place where they can work and live lightly together, sharing our skills and resources to realise our aspiration of "a good life for all" They hope to realise this through the development of eight live/work plots within a shared agricultural holding. Plotgate Venture is open to new members looking to actively participate in this process and discover their niche. Please contact through their Facebook page or **www.plotgate.org.uk**

- *Reforesting Scotland* journal (no.45 Spring/ Summer 2012): "Co-operative living – a low impact choice?"
  www.reforestingscotland.org/rs-journal-45

- Seeds for Change, useful help with info, training
  www.seedsforchange.org.uk

- Simon Dales' house
  www.beingsomewhere.net

- A Thousand Huts. Campaign to promote huts and hutting across Scotland– the building and enjoyment of simple structures (usually wooden) for living, working and recreation. "We want to achieve this by securing a change of culture and attitude and reform of the law so that those who wish to build huts and pursue hutting can do so freely and within the law." Launched in 2011 by Reforesting Scotland – a network which has campaigned for over 20 years for a sustainable forest culture in Scotland.
  www.thousandhuts.org
  www.reforestingscotland.org

- Tony Wrench's roundhouse
  www.thatroundhouse.info

and of course...

- The Diggers & Dreamers website features an online directory of intentional communities of all kinds within the UK. This includes just about all the low impact living communities mentioned in this book.
  www.diggersanddreamers.org.uk

9 780954 575748